D0962404

THE JUPITER EFFECT

THE
JUPITER EFFECT

JOHN R. GRIBBIN
and
STEPHEN H. PLAGEMANN

VINTAGE BOOKS
A Division of Random House
New York

VINTAGE BOOKS EDITION, May 1975, Revised 1976

Copyright © 1974, 1976 by John R. Gribbin and
Stephen H. Plagemann

Manufactured in the United States of America

Library of Congress Cataloging in Publication Data
Gribbin, John R
    The Jupiter effect.

    Reprint of the 1974 ed. published by Walker, New York.
    1. Earthquake prediction.   2. Earthquakes—
California.   I. Plagemann, Stephen H., joint author.
II. Title.
QE538.8.G74   1974b   551.1'3   74-26624
ISBN 0-394-71574-8

TO MINNA
*who told us to stop talking
and start writing*

Acknowledgments

The following illustrations originally appeared in the publications cited. We are most grateful to the publishers and authors of the original works for permission to reproduce them here.

Figures 1, 2, 3 and 4: from A. H. Cook, *Physics of the Earth and Planets,* Macmillan, London, 1973.

Figure 5: from *National Geographic Magazine,* January 1973.

Figure 7: from *Scientific American,* November 1971.

Figure 8: from C. R. Allen *et al.,* Relationship between seismicity and geologic structure in the California region, *Bull. Seism. Soc. Amer.,* **55** (1965), 753.

Figure 9: from Ll. S. Cluff, Urban development within the San Andreas fault system, in *Proceedings of Conference on Geologic Problems of San Andreas Fault System* (ed. W. R. Dickinson and A. Grantz), Stanford University Publ., vol. 11, Stanford, 1968.

Figures 10, 11 and 13: from R. A. Challinor, Variations in the rate of rotation of the Earth, *Science,* **172** (1971), 1022.

Figure 14: from W. A. Pomerantz and S. P. Duggal, Record-breaking cosmic ray storm stemming from solar activity in August 1972, *Nature,* **241** (1973), 331.

Figure 15: from E. Schatzman, The Earth–Moon

system, in *Interplanetary Torques* (ed. A. G. W. Cameron and B. G. Marsden), Plenum, N.Y., 1966.

Figure 17: from J. M. Wilcox and N. F. Ness, Quasi-stationary co-rotating structure in the interplanetary medium, *J. Geophys. Res.*, **70** (1965), 5793 © American Geophysical Union).

Figure 18: from K. D. Wood, Sunspots and planets, *Nature*, **240** (1972), 91.

Appendix B is reprinted from *New Scientist*, 27 December 1973, by courtesy of New Science Publications.

Contents

ACKNOWLEDGMENTS   vii

FOREWORD   xi

PREFACE   xvii

1 The geophysics of the San Andreas fault.   1

2 Plate tectonics and early history of the California fault system.   15

3 Detailed geology points to dangerous regions of the San Andreas fault.   30

4 Strain in rocks and fracturing experiments in the laboratory.   44

5 Earthquakes, the weather and changes in the Earth's rotation.   52

6 Do Earth tides trigger quakes?   71

7 How solar flares and cosmic rays affect the Earth's spin.   81

8 The physical links between the Sun and the Earth.   96

9 The solar sunspot cycle and alignment of the planets.   108

10 Preparation for the next great Californian earthquake.   133

APPENDIX A   Recent developments in earthquake
             prediction.   149

APPENDIX B   Our Weather: a link with the
             planets?   153

FURTHER READING   164

INDEX   177

Foreword

Everyone loves a mystery. It might be a fictional one—who stabbed the millionaire in his library when all the doors and windows were locked from the inside? It might be a historical one—who was The Man in the Iron Mask? Did a member of the Czar's family really escape the Bolshevik executioners?

But there are mysteries in science, too; mysteries that are far more cosmic in scope and much more immediately important to people. In science, too, there are detectives who gather inconsequential clues—clues far more tenuous than a trace of cigarette ash or a burnt match. There are people who weave chains of logic far more delicate and yet far more iron-bound than any put together by a Holmes or a Poirot.

This book is the story of one of those mysteries—that of the earthquake—and the lines of detection that now surround it.

In ancient times, the earthquake was but one more of the unaccountable disasters which the careless, whimsical or malevolent gods visited upon a suffering humanity. How could such a thing be predicted or forseen unless one could penetrate the mysterious mind of the immortals?

Some attempted to find a reason for earthquakes that was more nearly rational than the matter of divine whim. They suggested that vast giants, who had rebelled against the gods, were imprisoned in the ground and that their occasional writhings produced earthquakes and volcanic eruptions. But who can tell when a giant in his agony will writhe?

Others, abandoning the supernatural altogether, suggested that imprisoned air sometimes pushed against the imprisoning walls of rock and shook the Earth. This was getting closer but who could foretell where and when the next push would come?

Until modern times, however, interest in earthquakes was rather academic. Really bad ones occurred only rarely; the Earth was relative empty, and the works of man were small and easily rebuilt. As the Earth slowly filled, however, and the works of man grew larger and more intricate, the effect of earthquakes became more dreadful.

The turning point was on 1 November 1755 when a great earthquake, possibly the most violent of modern times, struck the city of Lisbon, Portugal, demolishing every house in the lower part of the city. Between that and a tsunami (or 'tidal wave') caused by the earthquake, 60,000 people were killed. The shock was felt over an area of 1,500,000 square miles.

The Age of Reason was then in full bloom, science was growing vigorously, and men looked upon earthquakes with new eyes. The English geologist, John Michell, suggested, in 1760, that earthquakes were waves set up by the shifting of masses of rock miles below the surface—and at last mankind was on the right track.

In 1855, the Italian physicist, Luigi Palmieri, devised the first seismograph, an instrument that was able to measure the slightest tremors in the Earth's crust. For the first time it became possible to track down the earthquake, calculate the spot at which it originated, the manner in which the waves it gave rise to passed through the Earth, and so on.

Since the seismograph was invented, earthquake studies have led to discoveries concerning the planet's inner structure that could not have been attained in any other way. Through the study of earthquake waves, for instance, we know that the Earth has a liquid nickel-iron core.

We know now those places where earthquakes most commonly occur. At first, though, there was no indication as to why the high-frequency zones occurred where they did. It was only in the last few decades that evidence was accumulated which indicated that the Earth's crust consisted of large 'tectonic plates'. These plates were pushed apart in some places by material that welled up from the Earth's deeper layers and were pushed together (in consequence) in other places. It was at the junction lines of these plates that the earthquakes occurred.

One of the junction lines is the San Andreas fault, which runs down the Pacific edge of California. There have been disastrous earthquakes along this fault before, notably in the San Francisco area in 1906. Each successive earthquake is enormously more damaging than the one before, moreover, because with each decade, California becomes more populous, more industrialized, and more full of the works of man.

When will the next quake come? If it cannot be stopped, may it not be possible to get out of the way (as much as we can) in time?

But the knowledge gathered concerning earthquakes in modern times—great though it is in volume and subtlety—still isn't sufficient to let us know just when one tectonic plate will scrape against another and set the crust to trembling. The plates are held motionless against each other by frictional forces, but the strain slowly increases from year to year and eventually some slight nudge will suffice to overcome the last scrap of the frictional hold and bring catastrophe in one fast, tearing, scraping slide. What produces the final nudge, though? Where does it come from? And when?

In this book, Drs. Gribbin and Plagemann are on the trail of that nudge, and it takes them not only over all the Earth, but to the Sun and through all the Solar System and even beyond.

Carefully, they lay out the clues and follow each of them in a fascinating chase that includes such things as tiny thousandth-second changes in the length of the day, and what might bring that about.

They consider explosions on the surface of the Sun that result in the speeding protons of the Solar wind and vaster explosions in distant space that result in the far more energetic protons of cosmic rays. What is their role?

They deal with tides in the solid body of the Earth, and tides in the Sun itself. And on that subject they come up with the strange influence of the positions of the planets in an odd (but *rational*) echo of astrological thinking.

And in the end, it turns out that something will happen in 1982 that just may—

No, no, read it for yourself. Read it carefully and you'll find it far more fascinating than the tale of any millionaire found stabbed in any library, locked or otherwise. And far more important, too—especially if you live in California.

ISAAC ASIMOV
17 April 1974

THE JUPITER EFFECT

Preface

Since the dawn of history, earthquake prediction has been the exclusive preserve of soothsayers and astrologers. Although the prophets of doom often caused alarm by spreading warnings about earthquakes which never in fact took place, they failed dismally to predict real disasters such as the San Francisco earthquake of 1906 or the Managuan earthquake of 1972. Over the past few years there has been a gradual change in this situation. Earthquake prediction has become a respectable branch of the earth sciences. As the new theory of plate tectonics has grown up, geophysicists have been able to explain why some regions are prone to earthquakes in terms of the movements of the plates which make up the surface of the Earth, jostling against one another like a stirred up jigsaw puzzle and carrying the continents on their backs. But even now the geophysicists cannot predict with accuracy when an earthquake will occur. At the time of writing (1973) it is, in fact, just becoming possible to predict the occurrence of certain kinds of earthquakes a few months ahead, and this exciting new work is discussed in Appendix A. But it is still fair to say that long-term prediction of major earthquakes is not possible within the strict confines of present geophysical knowledge.

Now, to the surprise of many scientists, there has come evidence that in one limited respect the astrologers were not so wrong after all; it seems that the alignments of the planets can, for sound scientific reasons, affect the behaviour of the Earth. The gravity of the planets can affect the Sun, through tidal interactions, and disturbances on the Sun can influence the Earth through changes in the magnetic field which links all the planets in the Solar System. Only on very rare occasions can these small effects add up to produce any dramatic results on Earth. But one of these occasions—an alignment of the planets which occurs only once every 179 years—is due in 1982. We are convinced that this will trigger off regions of earthquake activity on Earth, and by that time the Californian San Andreas fault system will be under considerable accumulated strain. Geophysicists report that their measurements of that fault now show that it is overdue for a slip greater than that of 1906, and just needs a trigger. There can be little doubt, we feel, that the planetary and solar influence in the early 1980s, following the rare planetary alignment, will provide that trigger. In particular, the Los Angeles region will, we believe, be subjected to the most massive earthquake experienced by a major center of population during this century.

Our purpose in writing this book is both to put forward the reasons for our firm belief in the imminence of the next major California earthquake, and also to warn the inhabitants of the region while indicating some ways in which the effects of this event can be lessened.

Since the publication of the original edition of this book in 1974 we have received valuable and interesting responses from many people, both for and against the ideas we have gathered together. Some of these responses have enabled us to make revisions which improve and update the material as presented in this edition; even taking account of work which has been put

forward over the past 18 months we are still, as of the
Spring of 1976, convinced that in broad outline at least
the effects we describe are real, and that our prediction
is as good as ever.

February 1976

J.G.
S.P.

1 The Geophysics of the San Andreas Fault

Plate Tectonics and World Earthquake Patterns

California is the most seismically active region of the forty-eight states (excluding Alaska and Hawaii) of the continental United States. This has been known for many years, and has important consequences for the region. California is the most populous of the states, a center of industry and commerce; in many ways it is the most important state of the union. Yet all this under the threat of repeated major earthquakes like the San Francisco disaster of 1906. Nearly seventy years after that earthquake, the human population seems literally to have cast from their minds any knowledge that their state could be laid waste by another serious tremor which would, of course, wreak more havoc with every year that passes, as population increases and society becomes increasingly dependent on industry. Perhaps this chosen path of ignorance was the best way, when even the most learned students of geology and geophysics did not know why California should be so prone to earthquakes—they were, it seemed, an act of God which no man could understand. If one came, well, just too bad.

But now the situation has changed. In the past decade there has been a revolution in the earth sciences which has brought a new understanding of our planet.

This revolution—as profound as the revolution in astronomy 500 years ago when Copernicus displaced the Earth from its position at the Center of the Universe—has resulted in a growing understanding of the forces which shape the continents and set them drifting about the world. Riding on the 'plates' of the Earth's crust which give the name to the theory of plate tectonics (figure 1), whose continents jostle against one another causing mountains to be thrown up, volcanoes to burst into fiery life, and earthquakes to occur. The events which seem so awesome to man, and make California one of the worst places in the world in which to make any long-term plans, are now seen as a visible manifestation of the processes which shape the continents. A part of California to the west of the San Andreas fault is simply riding on a different plate from the rest of the USA; rubbing shoulders with the continent as it drifts northwards at a rate of $3\frac{1}{2}$ to 5 cm per year. This fragment of continent occasionally sticks in one place for a few decades, only to be released with a jerk—a major earthquake—when the strain builds up sufficiently. But we are moving on too fast; just what is this theory of plate tectonics, and how has it revolutionized man's understanding of his terrestrial environment?

Continental Drift

The idea of continental drift has been around for a long time. According to this idea, the continents have reached the geographical positions we know today by drifting about the surface of the Earth like rafts floating on the molten rocks of the Earth's interior. In this drifting process the various rafts can bump together, making a certain distribution of continents, but within a few million years (a short time compared with the age of the Earth) they will be swept apart and rearranged in a new pattern of continents. The reason why the concept of continental drift became popular, even before there was convincing geological evidence that it occurs, is that when maps of the continent on either side of the Atlantic became available it was noticed that the shapes of continents seemed to be mirrored in the shapes of the corresponding coastlines on the other side of the ocean. This was first noticed in the case of Africa and South America, the most obvious 'fit' and, coincidentally, one of the first regions mapped in detail when seafarers left western Europe to explore the new world.

Francis Bacon commented on the similarity between the outlines of the coasts on either side of the South Atlantic Ocean back in 1620. Discussion about the cause of this similarity continued intermittently for the next two and a half centuries, but only at the end of the nineteenth and the beginning of the twentieth centuries did a real theory of continental drift emerge, to remain a source of controversy for decades. For while some geographers argued that similarities between the continents suggested that they were once joined in two supercontinents, Gondwanaland in the southern hemisphere and Laurasia in the northern, some geologists argued that there was no *physical* means by which the continents could have been made to drift around the globe. So the revival of the theory of continental drift some ten to fifteen years ago was the result of geophysical discoveries, most notably the fossil magnetism of continental rocks. There remain opponents of the theory today, but the consensus of opinion has swung behind continental drift.

Although the coastlines of, for example, Africa and South America look like mirror images on the map,

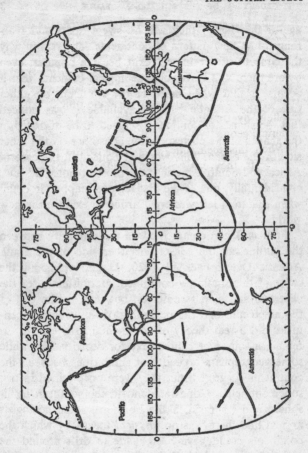

FIGURE 1. The continental jigsaw puzzle.

the exact coast depends on the height of sea level. When geophysicists are trying to fit pieces of the continental jigsaw together, they use the real edges of the continents—the edges of the continental shelf—as a guide (see figure 2). The shelf is only covered by a few hundred meters of sea, whereas the oceans are, on the average, about 4000 m deep. The first attempts at fitting continents together in this way were made by tracing the contours of the continental shelf and fitting them together by eye; now, with the advent of high-speed computers, the job can be done quickly and accurately by treating the problem exactly in terms of spherical geometry.

When this technique is applied to the present-day continents, they can be fitted together to form the supercontinents which geologists first suspected to exist some 200 years ago. But fitting together the edges of the continents is only half the story. It is the match of the geology of continents across these joins which provides even more impressive evidence. Similarities in rock strata and fossilized plants and animals, together with the continuation of mountain chains from one continent to another, all support the view that continents have been torn apart relatively recently in geological terms. For Africa and South America, the structures of northeast Brazil and West Africa fit almost perfectly to make up part of Gondwanaland. Other areas have not been studied in so much detail, but such evidence as there is again suggests that the two continents were joined about 550 million years ago. If this was not the case, then remarkably similar processes must have produced similar geological structures on the opposite sides of the Atlantic Ocean, without the ocean floor being affected in any way.

It is now possible to establish the date of the breakup of the supercontinent fairly accurately. An indication that West Africa and Brazil were separated at least 50 million years ago is provided by evidence of glaciation in the two continents, and also by fossil evidence preserved in the sediments laid down in river

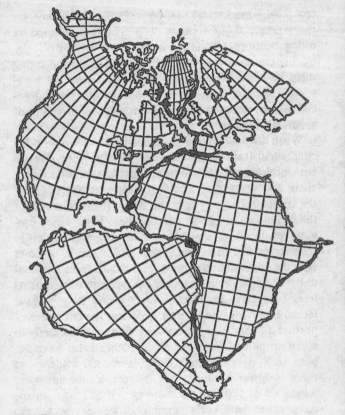

FIGURE 2. Continental Reconstruction (after Bullard *et al.* 1965).

basins along the margins of both continents. The remains found in both continents in sediments older than
about 100 million years are identical. At the end of the
Lower Cretaceous these freshwater deposits were covered by sea water which has left a layer of salt, and

since that time the similarities between the two continents' rock strata become less as the strata come nearer to the present time. So it seems fairly clear that the breakup of Africa and South America occurred between 100 and 200 million years ago.

What of the rest of the supercontinent of Gondwanaland which once dominated the southern hemisphere? Australia, Antarctica, Arabia, India, Madagascar and many of the smaller bits and pieces of Asian islands north of Australia can all be added to the South America–Africa supercontinent in much the same way, making up Gondwanaland. With so many pieces it is not possible to be sure that there were no inland seas in Gondwanaland (like the Black Sea today), and the position of some pieces of the puzzle remains uncertain. In particular, it is not clear whether India should be located against Australia or Antarctica. But on the whole the outline of Gondwanaland emerges well enough when the southern hemisphere jigsaw puzzle is put together.

In the northern hemisphere the corresponding jigsaw puzzle is simpler, having only three pieces—North America, Greenland and Eurasia. These pieces fit together to show the ancient supercontinent of Laurasia as it was 100 or more million years ago. These pieces of the jigsaw puzzle fit quite well if they are joined at the 500-fathom depth contour line, provided a few small pieces are left out. The most notable of these odd pieces are Iceland and the ocean ridges which rise up between Greenland and Europe—features which are, according to the geological evidence, less than 100 million years old and so could not have been present when the northern supercontinent of Laurasia existed. This agreement between the fit of the jigsaw puzzle and the age of the odd pieces is impressive; so too was the discovery that the Rockall Bank, a very shallow part of the North Atlantic which must be kept in when the jigsaw is reconstructed in order to fill a gap just north of Newfoundland, is really a submerged piece of continental crust much more than 100 million years old. So, rather more than 100 million years ago, the world contained just two supercontinents, Laurasia in the northern hemisphere and Gondwanaland in the southern.

Before that, a few hundred million years ago, these two supercontinents were probably joined together themselves, with all of the world's landmass concentrated in one super-supercontinent which geologists call Pangea. And before that? It is difficult to track the geological records so far back into the past, but the best idea, which agrees with such geological evidence as is available, is that before Pangea formed there were several continents, different from those we know today, which drifted together, whereas now the continents are drifting apart. When the Americas have crossed the Pacific and Australia drifts north into Asia, we will have the makings of a new Pangea. Will this in turn break up into smaller pieces, starting the cycle yet again? Or is this picture wrong in some way? The evidence already strongly hints at continental drift; however, one more piece of evidence was needed before the geophysicists were convinced.

Seafloor Spreading

Two vital discoveries led to the formulation of the idea of seafloor spreading, and both were made in the 1950s. First, when it became possible to use seismic reflection at sea, came the discovery that the Earth's crust is much thinner under the sea than it is under the continents. Typically, the underlying mantle of the Earth's interior lies only 5–7 km below sea level; the average distance below the surface of the continents is 33–35 km, but it can reach 80–90 km. This was discovered by measuring the time taken for sound waves from explosions to travel through the Earth's crust and upper mantle; explosives are set off at sea like dropping depth charges to destroy submarines and the echoes of the sound from the seafloor are recorded by hydrophones tens of kilometers away. From their experience of using the seismic technique on land—for example to find oil bearing rocks—geologists can calculate the thickness of the Earth's crust from the way it rings when the sound waves strike it.

Second, there came the very curious discovery that the world's oceans are split by a 'mid-ocean ridge'. The Atlantic Ocean's ridge, standing up to 3 km above the plains of the seafloor, really is in the middle of the ocean floor; it links to a ridge system which can be traced around the globe, and is associated with regions of earthquake activity; the mid-Atlantic ridge, for example, actually rises above the ocean surface at one point, forming the active volcanic island of Iceland. In other parts of the world the ridge is not in fact at the middle of the ocean, and today such ridges are more commonly called simply 'ocean ridges'.

In 1960 these two discoveries were put together in the first theory of seafloor spreading. Hot currents of molten rock in the Earth's interior could, it was argued, raise matter up to form the ridge systems. The thin crust typical of the ocean floors must be formed as this rising molten material solidifies and spreads out on either side of the ridge, pushing the thicker continental masses apart and forming the ocean basins of the world. From the dating of the break-up of Gondwana-land and Laurasia it seemed that spreading must have taken place at a rate of about 1 cm per year on either side of these ridges (so that the oceans grew wider at a rate of 2 cm per year) for hundreds of millions of years. At this rate all the ocean floor we know today could have formed in the past 200 million years—just about 5 per cent of the geological age of the Earth.

This leads to two equally intriguing possibilities. Either the Earth's surface has expanded by two-thirds— the proportion now covered by ocean—in that brief period of geological history, or old crust must be de- stroyed somewhere else, returning to the mantle to bal- ance the rate of creation of new crust. The first alter- native is not really consistent with the way in which the continents can be pieced together without much distortion on a globe the same size as the world today. But where could ocean crust be destroyed?

Ocean Trenches and the Magnetic Tape Recorder

Around the margins of the largest of the world's oceans, the Pacific, there is a series of very deep trenches. Could it be that these deep trenches are regions where the shallow crust of the oceans, pushed up against the thicker crust of the continents by the inexorable spread- ing of the seafloor, is forced downwards, returning to the mantle from which it once formed? The answer now seems almost certain to be 'Yes'. The picture widely accepted by geophysicists today is one in which the continents are more or less permanent features, carried on conveyor belts of oceanic crust which are continually reformed at ocean ridges and absorbed in deep ocean trenches like an escalator or moving pave- ment. The clincher which brought the body of scien- tific opinion behind this theory comes from a remarkable 'magnetic tape recorder' which has produced a picture of seafloor spreading almost as easy to read as a book.

When molten rock emerges from the Earth's interior and solidifies, magnetic components contained in the rock are aligned by the Earth's magnetic field while the rock hardens. Forever after, as long as the rock remains solid, it carries a fossil magnetism which indicates the direction of the Earth's magnetic field at the time when the molten rock was laid down. If the Earth's magnetism was steady and unvarying, this would be an interesting and useful geological tool but not a particularly remarkable one. However, when geologists drill cores from rock strata they obtain a historical record which shows, layer by layer, the history of rocks. To the surprise of many people, drill cores of rock strata from sites around the world all show that the Earth's magnetism has changed direction completely many times—north and south magnetic poles have 'flipped', replacing one another. The evidence for this is incontrovertible; as three successive layers of rock are laid down, it may be that one, laid down recently, carries the magnetic signature of the Earth as we know it today, while the next, a few million years old, is magnetized in the opposite sense, and the third, older still, is again magnetized in the same direction as modern rocks.

The cause of these sudden, dramatic changes in the Earth's magnetic field is uncertain. One suggestion— not a widely accepted one—which shows how desperate is the search for an explanation, is that they are caused by the repeated passage near the Earth of a strongly magnetic comet. There are better explanations, and the problem is being intensively studied, in particular at the University of Newcastle Upon Tyne. But that is another story, and for now let us be content, like most geophysicists, to use the evidence contained in magnetic rocks without worrying too much about how the magnetic poles of our planet can interchange.

Now, magnetic instruments can be towed behind ships to measure the magnetism of the seafloor below. When this is done, the records obtained show that the basalts which form the Earth's floor are magnetized

sea surface

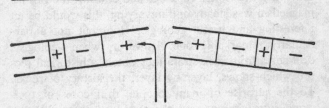

FIGURE 3. The magnetic tape recorder—seafloor spreading and magnetization: + rocks magnetized in present direction of the Earth's field;—rocks with reversed magnetization.

parallel to the Earth's magnetic field. But whereas the rocks nearest the ocean ridges are magnetized in the sense corresponding to the field today, those a little further from the ridges have the opposite magnetization, with repeated reversals as we look further and further away from the ridges. On either side of a ridge the pattern looks very similar to the pattern of reversals obtained by adding together information from core samples drilled on land and, perhaps most significant of all, the pattern on one side of a ridge is a mirror image of that on the other. (See the schematic representation in figure 3.) If these magnetic stripes were caused by the changes in the Earth's field they should form a historical record just like that of the cores drilled on land. Basalt solidifies at the ridge, carrying

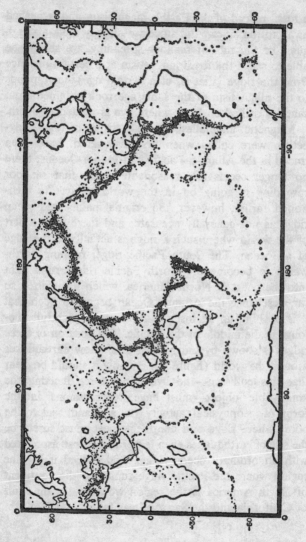

FIGURE 4. Worldwide distribution of shallow earthquakes.

a fossil record of the Earth's magnetism, and is pushed away to the sides. And since we already have a rough guess of the rate of seafloor spreading, we should be able to see if the fossil magnetism at a certain distance from the ridge (that is, of a certain age) corresponds to the magnetism of the same age rock obtained from samples drilled on land, where age is related to depth.

Magnetic 'anomalies', as these stripes of fossil magnetism were called when first discovered, have been traced in the Atlantic, Pacific and Indian Oceans; there no longer seems any reasonable doubt that seafloor spreading is going on in the world today. As mentioned earlier, however, the original name 'mid-ocean ridge' is not generally accurate; and there is one part of the world where such a ridge is actually at the edge of an ocean. The South Pacific ridge, running northwards to become the North Pacific ridge, runs right into the coast of North America, which has drifted so far west since the Atlantic Ocean began to open that it is pushing up against the ridge which rightfully belongs in the middle of the Pacific. The position of these ridges is shown by the pattern of shallow earthquakes around the world (figure 4). By now it should be clear that this collision—the irresistible force meeting the immovable object—must have repercussions in the form of geophysical activity on a grand scale. The point where ridge and continent meet must surely be the site of earthquakes even larger than those associated with an ordinary ocean ridge. And indeed it is. The region where the Pacific ridge runs into the continent of North America is the region we know as the Gulf of California and the San Andreas fault.

2 Plate Tectonics and Early History of the California Fault System

We have seen how giant conveyor belts carry the continents around the world, floating on top of the molten mantle rocks inside the Earth. This continental drift and the associated seafloor spreading, involving both the creation of oceanic crust at ocean ridges and its destruction in deep ocean trenches, is directly responsible for almost all of the earthquake activity around the world. The World-Wide Standardized Seismograph Network, set up in the 1960s to monitor earthquake activity, has made it possible to chart the occurrence of earthquakes and thus to trace the active regions around the world. These charts outline a series of plates—the pattern of seismic activity, traced on the globe, produces a jigsaw-like appearance (figure 4). Six or seven large plates fit together to cover the entire globe, and earthquakes are common where the plates touch. The magnetic tape recording of the seafloor basalts shows that these plates are moving relative to one another—jostling together or scraping side by side—and this is what causes the seismic activity.

The plates can, it seems, be made up entirely of oceanic crust or they may also contain permanent continental crust. But, as we have found, only the crust of the seafloor is involved in plate growth and destruction. Once new crust is formed, it remains part of a rigid plate until it is destroyed. This means that any distortion or deformation which takes place in the Earth's crust must happen at the boundaries of the plates, not in their central regions. Since the plates cover the entire globe, their movements must be mutual to some extent; when one plate moves it jostles its neighbors and a corresponding motion is produced in them. The motion of plates is complicated because, although on average the amount of new oceanic crust being created must balance the rate at which old crust is destroyed, at present there are more ridges from which crust grows than there are trenches via which it returns to the underlying magma. This means that the ridges themselves move relative to one another, and may be consumed by trenches. Other complications arise when continents are carried up against trenches—then the plate motions must change dramatically. Perhaps the most impressive remains of collisions in the distant past are the mountain chains of the continents, which seem to have been thrown up when pieces of continental crust collided. It is little wonder that the theory of plate tectonics has completely revolutionized geophysics, geo-chemistry and geology since the term was coined in 1967, and there is scope here for an epic story. However, for our present purpose we need only look in detail at one kind of collision between plates—the strike-slip interaction or faulting.

The American plate, on which the North American continent rides, is drifting in a direction just north of due west. The Pacific plate, on the other hand, is drifting in a northwesterly direction. As a result, the effect where the two plates meet is like a gigantic blow. If we imagine that the map in figure 1 (page 4) represents a jigsaw puzzle, the Pacific plate is twisting slightly anticlockwise relative to the American plate as if a giant hand were stirring up the pieces of the jigsaw puzzle. This disturbance is further complicated because the floor of the Pacific runs into America just where the strike-slip interaction is most pronounced.

So the San Andreas fault defines the boundary between the Pacific and American plates. Southwestern California is not part of the American plate at all, but is being carried northwest along with the rest of the Pacific plate on which it rides. From the magnetic recordings on the seafloor which have played such a large part in the development of plate tectonics theory, it is clear that America first ran into the Pacific ocean ridge system thirty million years ago. With the Pacific plate moving northwest at a rate of about 5 cm per year, it seems that when the interaction with the ridge began southwest California was about 1200 km further down the coast. These ideas can be tested by comparing the geology of northern Californian rocks with that of rocks from the west coast of Baja California, which was, thirty million years ago, the near neighbor of what is now northern California. At that time all of the area of California now to the southwest of the fault was to the south of today's border with Mexico.

Overall Features of the Present San Andreas Fault

From Eureka in the north down to the Gulf of California in the south, the complex maze of faults which can be traced through California runs, on average, from northwest to southeast, almost parallel to the Pacific coast and the mountains of the Sierra Nevada and the coast ranges. But, between Los Angeles and Santa Barbara, the San Gabriel mountains and associated faults strike east–west across the main line of Californian faults. Because of the plate motions already described, anyone looking across the main part of the fault system from the west would 'see' the rest of the states apparently moving right; equally someone looking across the faults from the east would 'see' California moving from left to right. For this reason the fault is described as 'right lateral'. But here again the Los Angeles–Santa Barbara region is an exception. There the Garlock Fault strikes east–west, dividing the Sierra Nevada from the Mojave Desert, and this is a left lateral fault—the desert moves to the east relative to the rest of California.

The great San Andreas fault itself, which is our main concern in this book, follows these overall trends closely. From San Francisco down to the southern end of the San Joaquin Valley the fault runs northwest–southeast; from the northern end of the Salton Sea depression to the Gulf of California the fault runs northwest–southeast. But in between, just west and north of the San Bernardino mountains, the fault bends sharply, running almost exactly east–west for a while (see figure 5).

This provides an important clue to the tectonic history of California and also, some experts argue, a hint as to the location of the next great earthquake. The big bend, as it is known, shows how southern California is being pushed around the San Bernardino Mountains—the not quite irresistible force of continental drift has come up against the almost immovable object of a mountain range, with dramatic consequences. For if the fault were straight, friction would make the movement of the two plates part each other in a series of jerks rather than a smooth slip. But because of the bend it is quite impossible for the American and Pacific plates to slide quietly past each other with only a little friction and a few small earthquakes.

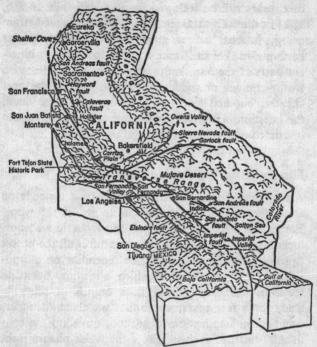

FIGURE 5. Thrusting ashore from the Gulf of California, the San Andreas fault system reaches almost to Oregon before vanishing beneath the Pacific. In addition to the master fault, there are hundreds of branch fractures. Major ones are shown here; all can cause quakes. Between Cholame and San Juan Batista, the sides fail to lock completely. Instead, they ease gradually past each other in a movement known as 'creep'.

Instead, progress must be made in a series of jerks because the knothole of the big bend resists the movement until so much tension has built up in the Pacific plate that it can jerk forward a few meters. Like the rest of the fault, the relative movement between the sides of the big bend region averages out at about 6 cm per year; but no movement at all for ten, twenty or a hundred years will be followed by a sudden shift of 0·6, 1, 2½ or 6 m. This sudden release of accumulated strain energy is what causes great damage and disastrous earthquakes. We shall take a closer look at how different parts of the San Andreas fault are associated with steady slipping or sudden occasional jerks in the next chapter; but first let us try to answer in some detail the question, 'How did the fault system reach the state it is in today?'

History of the Californian Fault System

A true insight into the San Andreas fault depends on an understanding of the plate tectonics of the whole Earth. The pieces of the global jigsaw puzzle are interlocked, and movement of one must affect all the others to some greater or lesser degree depending on the position and size of the piece which is moving. But plate tectonics has only existed as a branch of scientific study for a few years; we cannot yet claim to understand all the implications of seafloor spreading the continental drift, so we will ignore the wider picture from now on. Indeed we will also ignore the way in which the Californian fault systems connect and interact with the rest of the North American continent, although the effects of the collision between plates which produced the California we know today can be traced for thousands of kilometers inland. But even though we shall restrict our vision to the narrow view of the geological history of California, at the back of our minds we must be aware that the San Andreas fault is really just a minor feature of the interacting tectonic plates which make up the Earth's continental surface and seafloor.

The San Andreas fault itself seems to be made up of two zones. To the north comparison of the geology of the rocks on either side of the fault indicates that slip is taking place at a rate of only a centimeter or so a year, and has done so for several million years. In the south the slip is proceeding much faster, at about 6 cm per year. This is interesting but not a serious discrepancy. Presumably, over still longer periods of time, the average motion in both regions must be the same because both regions are part of the solid, steadily-moving Pacific plate. But even ten million years is a short time in geological terms, and a temporary difference between the speeds of slip in different parts of the fault might be explained if, for example, the North American plate is being stretched and bent over a wide region—if the two plates rub together more like two blocks of rubber than like two completely rigid plates. This leads to a very curious phenomenon, called elastic rebound, which makes the earthquakes which do occur much more serious than they might otherwise have been.

A simplified picture of what happens is shown in figure 6; if we imagine the two plates sliding past each other as shown by the arrows and then survey a line running at right angles to the fault line where the two plates meet, as shown in figure 6(a), we might guess that after some time the two plates will have moved so that our surveyed line will look like figure 6(b). But that does not happen. Because the edges of the two plates stick together, movement of the bulk of the plates away from the fault line causes the rocks to become stretched and distorted, as in figure 6(c). Eventually, of course, the stretch becomes so great that the rocks must snap along the fault line—but because they have been stretched the resulting whiplash, or rebound, shown in figure 6(d), takes them even further than they would have moved if the two plates had been slid-

ing smoothly past one another. This theory was first
formulated by Harry Reid in 1910, just four years after the famous San Francisco earthquake; for obvious
reasons the idea of slow accumulation of strain until
breaking point is reached is now known as Reid's elastic rebound theory. And it seems that the situation in
parts of California today is like that of figure 6(c).
But that is outside the scope of our look at the detailed
history of California, although we shall examine in
chapter 4 the details of the interaction on the boundaries of the Pacific and North Atlantic tectonic plates.

The two-part structure of the fault, and the big Los
Angeles bend, can be explained if the original Pacific
ridge, which America has now overrun, was also
sharply bent. This is more than likely. All the ocean

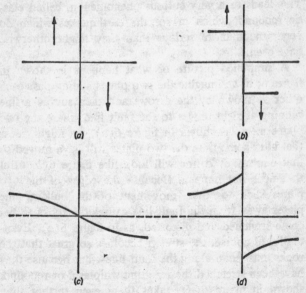

FIGURE 6. Simplified picure of elastic rebound.

ridges contain bends and breaks caused by detailed effects of the movements of the Earth's plates, and the former Pacific ridge should have been no exception. One possible scheme for the formation of California is outlined in figure 7. This should not be taken as the only possibility, or even the most likely, because it simply is not known exactly what happened thirty million years ago when North America overran the Pacific ridge system. But the broad outlines are probably correct.

In figure 7(b) we are looking at two adjacent strips of the Pacific floor, each spreading out on either side of the Pacific ridge but with a sharpish bend in the ridge system. Extending the analogy used before, we now have two conveyor belts running side by side. At an early age, as indicated in the top part of figure 7, there must have been a deep trench along the western seaboard of North America, like the trenches found today in the western Pacific near Japan. Seafloor created at the Pacific ridge was carried into that trench along the California coast and the crust was returned to the molten interior of our planet. Also, again like the situation today on the Japanese side of the Pacific, this descending seafloor would have pushed up against the bottom of the western coast of North America, causing earthquakes, volcanoes and a buildup of the mountain ranges which run from Alaska to the southern tip of South America. Scrapings from both the continent and the seafloor would accumulate in the region near the trench.

By the time the continental mass of North America reached the northerly part of the ridge shown in figure 7(b), both the ridge and the trench disappeared in that part of the conveyor belt system. The end of the Pacific plate which was pushed down into the mol-

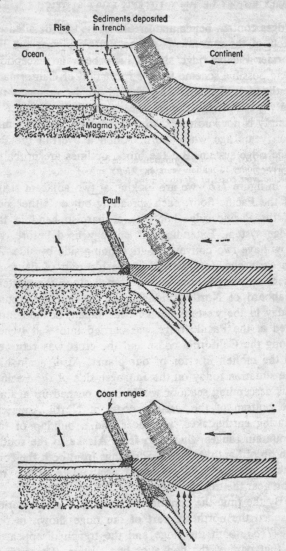

FIGURE 7(a)

FIGURE 7(a) *Opposite:* Interaction between rise and trench leads to mutual annihilation. The trench, formed as the oceanic plate dives under the continental plate, slowly fills with sediments carried by rivers and streams (*top*). Meanwhile the melting of the descending slab adds new material to the continent from below. When the axis of the rise reaches the edge of the continent, the flow of magma into the rift is cut off and trench sediments are scraped onto the western (that is, left) part of he oceanic plate (*middle*). The descending plate disappears under the continent and the sediments travel with the oceanic plate (*bottom*). The northern part of the San Andreas fault may have been formed in this way.

FIGURE 7(b) *overleaf:* Formation of the San Andreas fault system.
Top: Some 30 million years ago (*left*) an oceanic rise system lay off the west coast of North America, which was carried by a plate moving toward the rise crests. The continental plate overrides the Pacific plate, producing a long trench. Meanwhile the entire Pacific plate is moving northwest. After a few million years (*right*) the rise nearest the continent is shut off. The trench by now has been filled with material eroded from the continent. These deposits will later become the California Coast Ranges.

Centre: The northern section of the fault is created when the former trench deposits become attached to the northward-moving Pacific plate (*left*). The San Andreas fault lies between the two opposed arrows indicating relative plate motions. Meanwhile to the south a tilted rise crest (not visible in the first pair of diagrams) is ready to encounter the continent end on a break in the coastline south of Baja California. The collision (*right*) breaks off a part of the Baja California peninsula, which becomes attached to the Pacific plate and starts its journey to the northwest.

Bottom: The southern section of San Andreas fault is now fully activated (*left*) as the Baja California block begins sliding past the North Americn plate and collides with deeply rooted structures to the north, the Sierra Nevada and San Bernardino Mountains, which deflect the block to the west. More of Baja California breaks loose, opening up the Gulf of California. As Baja California continues to move northwestward (*right*) the Gulf of California steadily widens. The compression at the north end of the Baja California block creates the transverse ranges, which extend inland from the vicinity of present-day Santa Barbara.

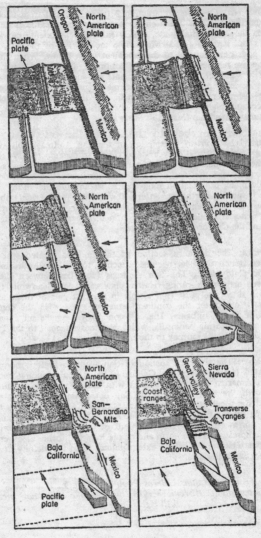

FIGURE 7(b)

ten magma broke off and, relieved of this weight, the rest of the plate pushed upward slightly, lifting up the sediment and scrapings in the former trench alongside the continent. These sediments are the stuff from which the coast ranges are made; the 'original' coast of America was alongside the Sierra Nevada mountains. Carried along on top of the Pacific plate, this new land began to slide northwesterly. Meanwhile, in the adjacent conveyor belt to the south, the interaction of trench and ridge was only just beginning. Baja California was still attached to the region which is now Mexico, the Gulf of California did not exist, and the rifting which produced the Salton Sea depression (about 60 m below sea level today) had not begun.

When the second of our two conveyor belts reached the North American continent, the ridge struck it obliquely south of Baja California. The spreading ridge has already driven into the continent like a knife, breaking off a sliver of land (Baja California) and opening out the Gulf of California. However, this entire spreading system will finally be subdued by the inexorable westward progression of the main mass of the North American continent. The most recent stage in this process could have been completed about only five million years ago, judging from the evidence recorded in the magnetic stripes of the ocean floor, when Baja California was still a part of the Pacific plate. As the peninsula was carried north by the movement of the plate, it collided with the main coast of North America near Los Angeles. Two important geological features result directly from this collision: First, Baja California is pivoting, as the northern end of this continental sliver is held against the San Bernardino mountains. This movement is opening the Gulf of California wider

and literally tearing the continent apart along the line
of the rift system which has produced a deep depression filled today by the Salton Sea. Second, great
blocks of the Earth's crust are being forced around the
knothole of the San Bernardino mountains, forming the
big bend of the San Andreas fault, where tectonic energy accumulates daily to be released only by the next
great California earthquake.

The horizontal scale of these movements is vividly
indicated by even a casual look at an atlas. Thirty million years ago the ridge and trench systems began to
interact, eliminating each other near San Francisco—
but at that time 'San Francisco' was about 1000 km
away near Ensenada in Baja California. Before the
creation of the Gulf of California 'San Francisco' was
part of the Pacific plate's seafloor. Vertical movements,
however, are less impressive than the horizontal motions of the Earth's crust. After all, the temporary oceanic crust, continuously formed at ridges and swal-
lowered up in trenches, is only a few tens of kilometers
thick, and even the permanent continental crust is only
a hundred kilometers or so thick—all that separates us
from the hot rock of the mantle is a layer no deeper
than the distance from San Francisco to Sacramento
as the crow flies. The distance between these two cities
today has changed in the past thirty million years;
San Francisco has moved by something between 450
and 900 km while in the past twenty million years,
Los Angeles has moved by around 200 km and Palo
Alto by about 3 km. Over that length of time the seismic activity associated with the movements of the Pacific and North American plates must have produced
thousands of great earthquakes in California and literally millions of small to moderate shocks. In geological

terms southern California is ten times more active seismically than the rest of the Earth; yet this part of the state contributes more than any other to the economic life of the USA.

3 Detailed Geology Points to Dangerous Regions of the San Andreas Fault

Now that we have sketched in the broad picture of global tectonics and seen how California reached its present state of geological activity, it is possible to see in perspective the economic and social consequence which this activity has. Historically, of course, man's knowledge about this aspect of his environment grew up in exactly the reverse direction. By piecing together information about seismically active regions around the world—information gained painstakingly by intense geological and seismic study, or heartbreakingly by observing major earthquakes and their consequences in populous regions—earth scientists have been able to paint the outline at least of the broader picture. Our discussion of seafloor spreading and plate tectonics was concerned with only very recent ideas, and rested upon very limited amounts of detailed information considering the area of the globe and the all-embracing scope of the theories. When it comes to geological details, the San Andreas and related faults provided almost an embarrassment of riches, dating back at least to the early nineteenth century reports of earthquakes in the area.

In order that we can see the overall picture of the San Andreas fault system, we shall have to look at some of the pieces in detail. From Cape Mendocino in the north to the Gulf of California in the south, the

San Andreas fault consists of three active regions separated by two quiet regions (figure 8). As we shall see this in an ominous quietness, hinting that these two regions are the likely candidates for sudden, catastrophic movement at long intervals. But first we will look in detail at the activity of one limited stretch of the fault containing both quiet and active regions. This provides a graphic illustration of what continental drift can mean over a length of time comparable to the lifespan of a man.

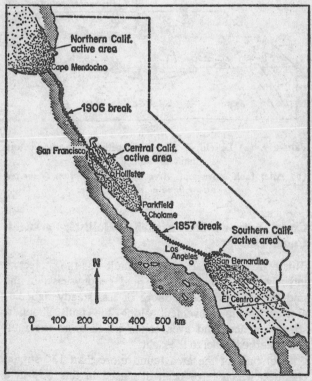

FIGURE 8. The San Andreas fault region.

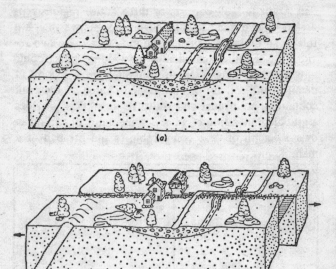

FIGURE 9. (a) Developed area along active fault trace before
fault movement.

(b) After fault movement. *Area of ground rupture is limited
to narrow band along fault trace.*

Creep Between San Francisco-Hollister-Parkfield-Camp Dix

This region of the San Andreas fault was the subject of
intensive study by geologists and geophysicists in the
mid-1960s. Evidence of more or less steady right lateral strike-slip movement along the fault abounds;
streams, fences and even roads which cross the fault
show marked kinks to the right.

One study of the area found more than 130 stream
channels which have been displaced in this way in a
110 km stretch of the fault. Forty of these have been

displaced by between 6 and 15 m, and many of the offsets are almost exactly 9 m (see figure 9). This common occurrence of a 9 m displacement may well be the result of the great earthquake of 1857 which was active in the region of this study. But the creep is, paradoxically, no cause for concern, at least as far as great earthquakes are concerned. It is a problem if you happen to own a road or gas pipe, say, which crosses these moving regions of the fault. But here tension is continually released, and there is no buildup of latent powerful forces waiting to be triggered into action and sweep all before them in a major, disastrous earthquake.

The stretch of fault between Cholame and Camp Dix has more preserved, conspicuously offset stream channels than any other similar length of the fault, which is why it was chosen for study. There is, of course, no doubt that this is the result of the slip in which we are interested. What we need to know is whether the fault is moving smoothly or in jerks, how big the jerks (if any) are, and how often the jerks take place. The stream channels alone cannot answer all of our questions, but they do give some important hints. If all of the 9 m shift found in about one-third of the 130 offset channels really was the result of the movement associated with the earthquake of 1857, then that was the largest strike-slip movment ever recorded in one single earthquake in modern times. Even larger offsets are seen in some of the streams, in one case 140 m, and in others more than 300 m. These must be the result of an accumulation of smaller offsets and continuous creep, so why should we accept that the 9 m offsets originated in one earthquake? Well, first of all there are so many offsets of around 9 m that it looks as if they were caused by one special event; second, if

there are not any offsets smaller than 6 m near the
9 cm offsets, what could they have been built up from?
On balance it looks as if offsets of 9 m can occur in
one strike-slip jerk of the San Andreas fault, and that
such movement occurred in the region between Los
Angeles and San Francisco in 1857, the last time that
a major earthquake was recorded in that area.

What other direct evidence of rapid slip in historic
times can we find? In many cases aerial photographs
clearly show an abrupt change in terrain from one side
of the fault to the other. That is useful information but
in itself it does not necessarily prove that the fault is
associated with horizontal movements rather than vertical fracturing of the Earth's crust. A combination of
aerial mapping to locate precisely the line of activity
and ground-based surveys of selected regions provides
the best insight into the activity of the fault. Using this
technique members of the United States Geological
Survey have investigated the 160 km of fault just to the
northwest of the region where classic examples of offset streams are found. Along this part of the fault, between Hollister and Parkfield to the east of Monterey,
the activity has recently been very different from the
activity along the fault just a few miles to the southeast.

This part of the fault seems to be quietly active today, and to have been so at least since 1906. Where
roads cross the fault line, the road surfaces show fractures corresponding to right lateral strike-slip of about
0·5 to 1 cm. Some of these fractures were very young
when the Geological Survey team carried out their
study; they are so small that during the summer, when
the asphalt softens, they are smoothed out when heavily loaded cattle trucks pass over them. It seems that
some of the cracks were certainly less than three

months old when surveyed in June of 1966—steady slip of up to $1 \cdot 25$ cm in three months (5 cm per year), just about in line with the average slip recorded in the rocks over geological ages of millions of years.

Perhaps one of the most widely noticed effects of such slip is the displacement of straight fences which cross the fault. All these movements agree with the right lateral slip which we know is a trademark of the San Andreas fault. The great value of such manmade objects is that we can be sure of the date on which they were erected, and we can be sure, too, that they were straight at that time. So it is a simple matter to work out the average rate of strike-slip movement. Between Cholame and Camp Dix, where dramatic 9 m offsets of stream channels are common, there is no evidence that roads and fences built in the past seventy years have been affected by the creep. Between the Cholame–Parkfield area and the Paicines–Hollister region such evidence of creep is common. For the whole of this Cholame–Hollister region the slip during this century averages out at just under $2 \cdot 5$ cm per year, though in the middle of the region the rate may be as much as 5 cm per year.

Further evidence of steady creep comes from within the city of Hollister, inland from Monterey Bay. Right lateral bending of sidewalks, pipelines, walls and other features can be seen along the fault line. In 1966 a sidewalk laid in 1910 and another laid in 1928 were observed to be shifted by the same amount (25 cm) as a gas pipeline laid in 1929. Presumably this means that there was little slip between 1910 and 1929 but that there has been slip averaging about $0 \cdot 7$ cm per year from 1929 to 1966. Another sidewalk built on a fault line shifted by 10 cm in the five years since 1966. The region between Cholame and Hollister is characterized

by complex and changing slip rates as tension is trans-
mitted between the San Andreas fault proper and the
Calaveras fault zone, which runs parallel to the San
Andreas fault a few miles further inland at this point.

What do these differing histories for adjacent parts
of the fault tell us? From Paicines to Cholame there
has been gradual creep for periods of at least years at a
time since the beginning of this century. South of Cholame to Camp Dix there has been no such gradual slip.
But there have been sudden, dramatic jerks (9 m in
1857) which add hundreds of metres of offset movement over the lifetimes of some streams in the area.
North of Cholame small earthquakes are not unusual
and have occurred several times in the past seventy
years, while to the south even the smallest seismic disturbances (micro-earthquakes) have been rare since
1857. The two regions north and south of Cholame
cover a particularly interesting region of the San Andreas fault, as they lie between the areas of extent of
the 1906 and 1857 earthquakes, yet overlap the outer
fringes of these great events. What do the differences
between these two regions tell us about the probable
location of the next great California earthquake?

There are two obvious possibilities: either the region between the two great earthquakes is now adjust-
ing more gently to the movement they each achieve so
dramatically, or the two now quiescent regions are lag-
ging behind the overall movement of the part of California attached to the Pacific plate. From the information gathered already in this and preceding chapters,
it is possible to make a good informed guess as to
which of these two alternatives is the more plausible.
We can make the choice even more certain, however,
by stepping back again from the detail of the fault
north and south of Cholame and taking another look at

the entire wood—the fault system from Cape Mendocino to the Gulf of California—bearing in mind what
we have learned from our close inspection of a couple
of typical trees.

Patterns of Active and Inactive Regions Along the San Andreas Fault

The small region of the fault which we have examined
in detail is a microcosm of the whole San Andreas system. Our aim is either to predict when and where the
next great Californian earthquake will occur, or, more
modestly, to define regions of the fault which are likely
to move in large, sudden jerks and to indicate roughly
the times when such areas of the fault will be particularly prone to sudden strike-slip movement. Many geologists have pointed out that throughout the length of
the San Andreas fault there is no correlation between
areas where there is now a great deal of small to me-
dium-scale seismic activity and areas in which disastrous earthquakes have occurred in the past couple of
centuries. Indeed, there is an *anticorrelation;* for in
the case of the San Francisco–Camp Dix segment of
the fault, the 'great' earthquakes have occurred in regions which today are the least active seismically.
Along the fault line there are regions which show every
variety of strike-slip motion from continuous creep to
occasional great earthquakes. Are these conditions permanent features of particular regions of the fault? And
if so, can we use the ever growing pool of geological
knowledge about the San Andreas fault to predict
which segments will suffer great earthquakes? If this
is the case, then half of our prediction problem will be
solved. It seems that insight into the nature and the
release of strain in rocks has now provided an affirma-

tive answer to both questions, with the proviso, of
course, that by 'permanent' we mean such features that
last for many human lifetimes. In the $4\frac{1}{2}$ billion year
history of the Earth, the California fault system—and
indeed California itself—can only be regarded as tran-
sitory, insignificant features.

Because so much evidence has now been accumulated showing how large displacements result from
continuous creep, and since fairly large horizontal
movements occur along a strike-slip fault even during
a quite small earthquake—such as the San Fernando
earthquake of 1971—there is certainly no need to expect that great earthquakes must occur everywhere
along the fault line. Indeed smaller-scale, more frequent movements are so effective in relieving strain
along much of the San Andreas fault that it could well
be that regions of great earthquake activity, rather
than repeated small earthquakes, are the exception
rather than the rule. Not only are two particular sections of the San Andreas fault now completely quiet—
as seismically inactive as the most stable continental
landmasses—but they are geologically distinct from
the three active regions of the fault.

The Danger Areas and Future Large Quakes in California

What exactly happened, geologically speaking, during
the two great earthquakes of 1857 and 1906? South of
San Bernardino the situation is very confused. What has
happened here is that Baja California has run up
against the obstacle of the San Gabriel mountain
ranges during the course of its drift to the north. Something has to give as a result of this collision, and the
thin continental crust north of the Gulf of California is

being crumpled and torn apart as the mountains deflect the northward-moving Baja California peninsula to the west. The simple fault line is replaced by a many-branched fault system, which is active today in the form of repeated small-scale earthquakes and creep like the events north of San Francisco. In other words, the area is safe as far as great earthquakes are concerned.

San Bernardino–Parkfield Region (1857 Quake)

Between San Bernardino, just east of Los Angeles, and Cholame, just south of Parkfield, the situation is very different. Of course the 1857 event is less well documented than the San Francisco disaster of this century, but it seems fairly clear that the break in the fault ran for at least 350 km, from Cholame to San Bernardino (see figure 8, page 31). Along this line the fault shows up clearly as one continuous line. Northwest from San Bernardino there are no breaks or branches of any importance in the fault until we get to Cholame. There we find that the fault has been jogged sideways by about 1 km, and the Cholame valley forms a distinctive feature in the landscape, surrounded by much rougher terrain. Significantly there is also a clearcut change in the type of underlying rocks beneath the terrain near Cholame. The rocks adjacent to the fault but northwest of Cholame were, it seems, laid down under different conditions from those which form the 'basement' adjacent to the fault but southeast of Cholame.

San Francisco–Cape Mendocino Region (1906 Quake)

Much of this evidence was gathered together from various sources a few years ago by Dr. Clarence Allen of the California Institute of Technology. Dr. Allen was concerned with the 1906 break in the fault, and although a large part of this break is underwater it does seem that there are many similarities between the two quiet danger regions. At the southern end of the 1906 break, near Hollister, the fault branches into the complex Calaveras–Hayward fault system which runs roughly parallel to the coast just inland from San Francisco Bay. North from Hollister to Cape Mendocino the fault is again a single, simple break, while beyond Cape Mendocino the magnetic recordings on the seafloor show a confused jumble of complex fault branches. While both the 1857 break and the 1906 break show a pronounced bend in the middle, the rocks northward of the 1906 break are typical of the seafloor and somewhat different from those adjacent to the fault just south of Cape Mendocino.

All of this evidence points to the likelihood that these two segments of the fault are the locations of occasional great earthquakes which release the accumulated strain of decades in one jerk. Perhaps the bends in these two regions of the fault help to lock the fault in one place while the strain builds up. Both segments are free from side branches which elsewhere are associated with frequent minor activity. In the other three segments, however, the geology is such that it seems almost certain that they never experience truly great earthquakes. Strain is gradually released by creep and small seismic disturbances almost as quickly as it accumulates. All these features seem to be permanent in the sense that they have existed for thousands of years (during the whole of the recent epoch of geological time) and will continue substantially unaltered during the foreseeable future of mankind.

To some extent the 'quiet' and 'active' parts of the fault overlap. The San Francisco region is the best example of this, and San Franciscans seem to get the worst of both worlds because the San Andreas fault runs down into a region where small-scale, repeated activity is produced by movement of the system of faults including the Calaveras–Hayward (see figure 8, page 31). But this exception does not detract from the overall significance of the discovery that the fault as a whole divides into regions where minor activity is common and regions where strain can only be released in occasional great earthquakes.

It seems, then, that we can answer the question, 'Where in California will the next great earthquake occur?' If only two regions of the fault are susceptible to great earthquakes, and if strain builds up at a fairly steady rate along the entire fault, then the region of the great earthquake *before* the most recent disaster is the most likely candidate for the next such event. The naive guess that seismically quiet regions are the safest does not stand up for the case of the San Andreas fault.

Along the northern segment of fault corresponding to the 1906 earthquake, strain has accumulated unrelieved for nearly seventy years, and if it could be realized the fault would presumably slip by 70×6 cm, or $4 \cdot 2$ m. But along the line of the 1857 slip, strain has been building up, presumably at the same rate, for getting on for 120 years. This corresponds to an impending slip of $7 \cdot 2$ m—and we already know from evidence of offset stream channels that the 1857 earthquake itself produced a slip very comparable to this size, about 9m. These figures have an ominous look; after all, the common sense guess would be that in 1857 accumulated strain was released when strain built up to 9 m of slip stored in rocks. There is no reason to believe that the forces holding up the slip today are any different from what they were in the last century. It may be that the 1857 segment will slip again when another 9 m of stored-up strike-slip overcomes the restraining forces, which gives us until 2001 to prepare for the next great earthquake. But it would not be surprising to see the fault jerk at any moment, especially if some outside influence provided an extra push to trigger the jerk.

So our second question 'When will the next great earthquake occur?' assumes an immediate practical importance. This is no hypothetical question to pass on to our children and grandchildren. We can be pretty sure that the slip will come within our lifetime, that it will be roughly as great as the slip of 1857, and that unlike the situation in the mid-nineteenth century it will affect one of the most densely populated regions of the state. Los Angeles will soon find that the San Fernando earthquake of 1971, which was produced by movement on a small fault a little way from the San Andreas fault, was small beer as California earthquakes go in spite of the destruction it caused. But how accurately can we pin down the date of the next major slip? Factors affecting the whole of the globe, rather than the activity of one small region, could easily provide a trigger for the San Andreas fault and we shall see that such factors come to a head early in the 1980s. Time may be even shorter than we have guessed. But before we move back again to look at the global picture—and indeed at processes which make the Earth itself an insignificant mote in space—we will first see just how strain in rocks can be tolerated up to a certain point, but above that point the rocks can no longer contain the forces on them.

4 Strain in Rocks and Fracturing Experiments in the Laboratory

When we begin to look at the detailed physics of fracturing in rocks, and the physical processes which go on when pieces of rock on either side of a fault slip past one another, we are leaving the solid ground of physics far behind. The kind of mechanics which we are taught in high school and college—the perfect elastic solid which obeys Hooke's law or the ideal viscous fluid which is incompressible and has no internal friction or viscosity as described in detail long ago by Newton—is concerned largely with 'perfect' examples. The laws of physics are clearly laid down in this area of classical mechanics, and by following the rules it is a straightforward matter to calculate what will happen to an object when a certain force is applied to it in a certain way. The Hooke solid exhibits a simple proportional relation between stress and strain.

But real life is nowhere near as simple, and the behaviour of rocks under the conditions which we find along the San Andreas fault is far from being the simplest problem in the real world. Helpful pieces of information about the effects of pressure on fractured rocks can be gleaned both from the laboratory experiments which have been carried out on rock samples and from geological studies in the field. In both types of empirical study we shall be concerned with rules of thumb which have no foundation in any comprehensive theory of the structure and behaviour of rock. To take a rather way-out example of an empirical rule, it is well known that every President of the USA elected during a year which completes a decade (Kennedy in 1960, Roosevelt in 1940 and so on at twenty-year intervals) has died in office, albeit after serving one, two or three terms. There is no logical explanation for this; but would you run for President in 1980? Getting back to more or less solid ground, the empirical 'rules' concerning the behaviour of rocks under pressure seems to come part way between an ideal elastic solid and an ideal viscous fluid. Logically enough they are described as being viscoelastic.

The study of viscoelasticity in rocks is concerned with low temperatures and pressures—conditions which we shall find are curiously appropriate for the San Andreas fault although quite inappropriate as a guide to the activity of most earthquake regions around the world. This is because the jerks which are associated with very large earthquakes only occur where the two plates of the Earth's crust are locked together temporarily. At great depths, where temperature and pressure are both high, it seems that the plates slide past one another smoothly throughout the length of their line of contact. In other words California's earthquakes are all shallow focus, occurring at depths where temperature and pressure are relatively low and the empirical theory of viscoelasticity can be applied, at least roughly.

Experimental studies of rocks in the laboratory have been carried out by many teams, notable among them the various groups of the United States Geological Survey. Under pressure some rocks become plastic; that is the rocks stretch elastically until some critical yield stress is reached, and then suddenly slip irreversibly along fracture zones. This happens only under particular conditions—when the temperature is high and the strain on the rocks is slow and steady. The exact behaviour of these rocks also depends on their previous history of fracture and faulting, but the empirical rules worked out so far are much too crude to take account of this in any reliable way.

The important factors which affect the flow and creep of real rocks are the amount of stress and the rate at which the stress is applied. If a small stress is applied for a short time, the rock will be deformed but can spring back elastically to its original position when the stress is removed; recovery of this kind occurs in small to medium flow and fracture. After large-scale flow or fracture, however, the rock is distorted to breaking point by large stress over long periods of time and cannot return to its original position. Naturally, all these effects—fracturing, elastic deformation, flow and recovery—are combined in various proportions in real rocks; but the general effects can be differentiated as clearly as can the active and quiet fault regions of California.

For our present purpose, the phenomenon of creep is the most interesting example of the behaviour of rocks under stress. Fracturing is an example of the effect of creep; as stress increases, the strain *across* a fracture (like the San Andreas fault) increases even more rapidly than the stress along the fracture. Eventually rock samples exposed to sufficient pressure are split apart. This is how some of the complex fault and fracture systems associated with the San Andreas fault may have grown up. These and other processes of creep are well documented in a general way, but the rather empirical studies of viscosity and elasticity are inadequate to describe what is going on mathematically. When it comes to predicting the behaviour of rocks under stress we must fall back on laboratory experiments and field studies. Even though there are no equations to describe in detail what happens to deformed rocks, one fact of great importance emerges from the laboratory studies. Like the straw that broke the camel's back, when the conditions are right the addition of a very small extra stress can act as a trigger to relieve strain by deforming the rock rapidly over a wide area. This is directly applicable to the San Andreas fault and provides further strong support, if any were needed, for the idea that the regions of the fault which are quiet and subject to huge long-term stresses are just those regions most likely to suffer catastrophic earthquakes. Knowing that strain is now building to a peak in parts of California, all we need to predict when the catastrophe will occur is to find the trigger—but that is a pretty big proviso which has baffled many people.

Before we look for the trigger mechanism, we can see how laboratory tests provide a very clear understanding of one feature of the California shallow-focus earthquakes which was, until a couple of years ago, baffling to both geologists and geophysicists. The depth at which Californian earthquakes originated is only 10 or 20 km below the Earth's surface. But the tectonic plates which are sliding past each other on either side of the San Andreas fault are, according to the best geophysical evidence, several times thicker than this. Shouldn't there be disturbances right down to the bottom of the plates? The best way out of this dilemma is to postulate that below a certain critical depth the motion of the plates is a smooth creep, while the jerks and lurches occur closer to the surface. Both this kind of uneven motion—'stick-slip'—and smooth fault creep are found when rocks are subjected to high pressure in the laboratory. What causes one kind of motion to be preferred over the other? The answer—or at least one important factor—may well be the temperature of the rocks, according to a study carried out by Dr. W. F. Brace of the Massachusetts Institute of Technology, and Dr. J. D. Byerlee of the United States Geological Survey.

The reason why so few experiments on frictional sliding of rocks at high temperature and pressure have been carried out is that not only must the rock being tested be kept in a hot environment, but the container must also be large enough to allow the rock to distort as sliding along fault lines occurs. Once these experimental problems were overcome a detailed picture of the combined effects of temperature and pressure on friction in rocks began to emerge. Drs. Brace and Byerlee used cylindrical samples of rock to try and find out what happened to faults at different temperatures and pressures. Unfortunately faults are hard to come by, in laboratory-sized pieces of rock at least, so quite often sawcuts were used as artificial faults. This raised some difficulties in interpreting the results of the experiments. Sawcuts are flat, with finely ground surfaces; each sawcut is almost identical with every other. On the other hand real fractures are rough; their surfaces are irregular and one fracture can be very different from another. In spite of these difficulties the experiments on sawcuts were useful when compared to the few experiments carried out on real fractures. There is more 'scatter' in the results for fractures but the data on fracture is in the same ball park as the results for sawcuts. Since we are only concerned with general properties, these experiments provide a useful insight into the influence of high temperatures on fractures.

The experiments were carried out on both granite and gabbro. Both are igneous rocks born from the molten magma of the Earth's interior, and both are coarse-grained rocks. Gabbro is composed of pyroxene, hornblende and biotite, while granite contains potassium feldspar and quartz, with only small amounts of biotite and hornblende. More important from our point of view, both are characteristic of rock strata underlying California. The pressures used in the experiment ranged up to 5000 bar (1 atmosphere pressure $= 10^{-1}$ bar $= 10^{+6}$ dyne cm^{-2}) and the temperatures went up to 500°C. For both kinds of rock high temperatures profoundly influenced stick-slip sliding; it was replaced by stable sliding as the temperature increased. The transition from one kind of sliding to the other is more pronounced for sawcuts than for real faulted rock samples, but it is still revealed by the experiments. There is no physical explanation of this transition at high temperatures in faulted rocks—it is an empirical result. In many ways the experiments provide only an incomplete guide to the behaviour of fault systems such as those in California. For example, the presence of debris in the fracture has a pronounced effect. Sawcuts are free from debris, and undergo stick-slip at pressures of only a few hundred bars. For a fault in granite containing a little debris, the critical pressure for stick-slip movement is raised to more than 1000 bar, and for crushed granite—all debris and no crystalline rock—stick-slip begins only when the pressure reaches 8000 bar.

There is also the problem of water in the rocks. Water can act as a lubricant for faults, encouraging earthquakes. Geophysicists discovered this (empirically!) when the us Army pumped waste material from chemical and biological weapon manufacture down a well in the Denver area in 1963; a few years later the discovery was confirmed when an oil company in Colorado pumped water into the ground in order to push oil towards the surface and minor earthquakes began at one side of the oil field. Geologists from the National Center for Earthquake Research were called in, and when they pumped the water out of the ground the earthquakes stopped. Now water has been pumped into the ground yet again, and earthquakes—on a small scale—have restarted. The first tiny step towards artificial earthquake generation has been taken. Getting back to California, however, the question of the water content of the rocks remains an unknown to confuse the application of the results of laboratory experiments to the real world. Also, the strain on rocks 'in the field' is slower and more steady than it was in the laboratory tests—the experimenters obviously could not wait for tens or hundreds of years to complete experiments or watch the slip of the faults.

But even with these caveats it does seem 'that the disappearance of earthquakes at shallow depth in California could well be due to increased temperature', as Drs. Brace and Byerlee put it. At a depth of 15 km the temperature of the Earth is between 300°C and 500°C, just in the range of the temperature boundary between stick-slip and steady slip found in the laboratory. Just as the geologists working with the Colorado field are beginning to understand how to lubricate faults, so the laboratory experiments are beginning to give insight into overall features of fault movements. Our search for an understanding of the San Andreas fault has so far taken us from the global arena of plate tectonics down to the detailed geology of the fault itself and finally to high pressure and temperature experiments on small samples of rock in the laboratory. To find a trigger for the incipient jerk which we have found to be locked up in parts of the fault we must again start from an overall pciture of the Earth, as well as looking outwards to the Sun and the Solar System where processes far more violent than all the seismic activity on Earth are going on and may reach out soon to jolt our planet, shaking the San Andreas fault back into life.

5 Earthquakes, the Weather and Changes in the Earth's Rotation

All the San Andreas fault needs to lurch into life is a small nudge. Even so no influence of man is strong enough to provide the necessary nudge, unless some fool takes it into his head to pump water down a deep well near the locked sections of the fault, or a nuclear device is exploded underground in the western part of the state of California. Indeed, from what we have seen of the overall worldwide pattern of plate tectonics and the intimate way in which the motions of the plates which make up the Earth's crust are related, it seems most unlikely that any sort of local disturbance will be the trigger of the next great Californian earthquake. Instead we should begin to think of disturbances of the margin of these tectonic plates. Is there any event, or combined series of events, which might trigger a shaking of these boundary regions and cause a ripple of seismic activity around the earthquake-prone regions of the globe?

Even as recently as ten or twenty years ago, anyone who argued that the spin of the Earth was slowed down and speeded up, like that of a top, by routine events in the Solar System, would have been classed as a crank. Indeed, any contemporary of this 'crank' who professed a belief in the theory of continental drift would have been unlikely to obtain a teaching post in a good university in the United States. Now, it is often said that you cannot become a professor of geophysics in America unless you do profess a belief in continental drift; and although the situation is not quite the same for those who study the interactions of the Earth, the Sun and the planets, at least the climate has warmed sufficiently so that their views are discussed and published in the respectable scientific literature. Just how respectable these once scorned ideas are will be seen later; first, how might patterns in the overall seismic activity of our planet give us clues as to how earthquakes are triggered in the San Andreas fault?

Earthquakes, Chandler Wobble, and Movement of the Earth's Poles

As the Earth spins on its axis and follows its elliptical path around the Sun, its axis of rotation wobbles like a child's top, and for precisely the same reason. Like the child's top, the Earth is not exactly spherical. The Earth bulges out around the equator and this equatorial bulge provides a 'handle' whereby the gravitational fields of the Sun and Moon can get a grip on the Earth and disturb its smooth passage through space. Most people know that the Earth's pole does not always point to the same point in space—that is, to observers living on Earth the patterns of the constellations seem to wheel around with a period of 25,800 years. What is really happening is that during that time the Earth's axis traces a circle on the sky of about 47 degrees of arc. Today Polaris lies almost exactly above the North Pole, and by the year 2000 AD Polaris will be a still better pole star; by about 14,000 AD, any people still living on the Earth will be using Vega as their pole star. One interesting side-effect of this precession is that the definition of star coordinates, which astronomers use to locate stars (in much the same way that we chart places on the Earth by their latitude and longitude), must always be defined by reference to a certain year. One set of standard coordinates was defined in 1920; by 1950 these differed so much from the real sky that a new standard was introduced, and today some astronomers use a coordinate system based on the 1980 position of the stars. All of these changes, from the long-term change, over many thousands of years, of the Pole Star to the humdrum routine of standard astronomical measurements, result mainly from the precession of the Earth caused by variable gravitational pull of the Sun and the Moon on the Earth's equatorial bulge.

Since the Moon's orbit does not follow a simple circle around the equator, the effect of its changing gravitational field produces a secondary nodding effect in the movement of the Earth's spin relative to the fixed stars. This affect, known as nutation, is much smaller in amplitude than the 25,000-year precession and it has a period of only 18·6 years. Astronomers have known about nutation since 1747; but it is not the end of the story. Yet another, more frequent kind of polar wandering is known, named the Chandler Wobble after the amateur American scientist who first described it in 1891. This wobble is a motion of the pole with respect to the crust, and differs from nutation, which is a movement of the pole with respect to the fixed stars. Unlike the other two effects, however, the source of this 'dance of the pole with respect to the crust' is well known to be a free oscillation with a 14-month period. The best ideas today link the Chandler Wobble to the occurrence of magnetic forces which cause the molten core inside the Earth and the surrounding rigid crust to affect one another, and to the occurrence of earthquakes in the rigid crust. The wobble should also show lunar and solar tidal frequencies due to asymmetry of continent and oceans, but the effect is too small. However, because of the 'responsiveness' of rocks to these tidal periods, they may be important for triggering earthquakes (see chapter 6).

There is a very real 'chicken and egg' problem when it comes to investigating the relation between the Earth's wobble and earthquakes. It is not difficult to find that some changes in the wobble coincide with earthquake events. Thus the seismologist would tend to say that the Earth wobbles and that this shakes earthquakes into action; while the astronomer may say that earthquakes cause large shifts in the mass distribution of crust in the outer parts of the globe and such redistributions cause the polar axis of the Earth to wobble. In fact both points of view are probably correct. Wobble, changes in the length of the day, and earthquakes must interact in a complex way, with changes in one affecting the other and then producing a feedback upon the original changes. But in the past two or three years earth scientists have begun to get a better handle on some aspects of this complex interaction.

One recent study, by Drs. Mansinha and Smylie of the University of Western Ontario in Canada, concentrated on the effect of the large shifts in the mass distribution of crust involved in great earthquakes, upon the motion of the Earth's axis of rotation. First, the relatively steady parts of the polar motion (called the secular shift) are separated in order to distinguish them from the wobble. Both secular shift and wobble have been monitored by astronomical observations at a specially created worldwide network of stations. This network has been in operation for all but a few years of this century, and from this accumulated evidence it seems that from time to time something energizes the Chandler Wobble to produce a regular change in the direction of the axis of rotation. This occurs with a period of about fourteen months and an amplitude which dies away after ten to thirty years. What could be the mechanism which excites this wobble?

One idea which received widespread support is that the seasonal movement of large masses of air around the globe could produce an effect with a period of about one year. However, this idea does not stand up to detailed examination—after all, the period of the Chandler Wobble is not *exactly* one year—but it is worth remembering that the motions of very large air masses affect the behaviour of other parts of the complex system which makes up the Earth as we know it. We shall see that shifting air masses play a role in other theories bearing on the question of earthquake prediction, since they occur over a period of a few days when a rapid change of stress can weaken rocks. Indeed, Dr. Donald Anderson at Cal Tech has shown that the high correlation between irregular (in 10 years) variations in the length of the day, Chandler Wobble amplitudes and global seismic activity may be partially due to climactic changes and ultimately to explosive activity. It should be added that he believes these correlations are attributable to random internal changes within the Earth itself rather than to the weather and solar phenomena. One of the greatest changes of the length of the day noted by Anderson and the related burst in large earthquakes occurred around the beginning of the twentieth century when California's most devastating quake rocked the city of San Francisco. In addition, we should note the research of Dr. C. Sugawa and his Japanese colleagues who show the physics of a strong correlation between solar activity, the atmosphere and changes in the rotation of the Earth. Their patient collection of data at the Mizusawa Latitude Observatory has paid off handsomely in terms of increasing our understanding of the Earth's atmosphere and solar activity.

The best idea now available is that the wobble is excited not by motions in the atmosphere above our heads, but by changes in the Earth beneath our feet. According to detailed calculations made by Drs. Mansinha and Smylie (and similar work by other people) there is enough energy involved in a sudden large-scale movement of a great fault like the San Andreas to provide the impetus for the wobble. In addition, the historical records indicate that there were measurable changes in the pole position at the time of at least four great earthquakes in this century, including the San Francisco disaster of 18 April 1906. The cause and effect relation is certainly not definitely proved, as Dr. F. A. Dahlen points out, but earthquakes are a possible source of the Chandler Wobble. Although it might seem that we are looking in the wrong direction for something to trigger earthquakes, at least this evidence shows that we have found an interesting trail—earthquakes and the wandering behavior of the spinning top we live on are part of the same story. If we turn away from the particular trail of the Chandler Wobble and look at irregular fluctuations in the spin rate of the Earth, we shall find that the story becomes still more intriguing.

Changes in the Rate at which the Earth Spins

The speed with which the Earth turns on its axis is not steady. Variations in this speed, and the resulting changes in the length of day (for one day is simply the time taken for the Earth to turn on its axis once) can be divided into three groups. First, there is a slow but steady increase in the length of day. This slowing of the Earth's rotation is the result of lunar and solar gravitational effects, and is continuing all the time at a rate of 0·0016 seconds per century. However, it is important to note these tidal influences are not constant over the Earth, but vary mainly with a well-known twelve-hour period. The long-term effect of the apparent motion of the Moon on the Earth was noticed by Edmund Halley (of comet fame) back in 1695, although he thought then that the Moon was speeding up, rather than the Earth slowing down. Second, there is an annual and semi-annual seasonal variation in the length of day, and the amount of this variation itself changes from year to year. All other affects aside, a day in Spring is about 0·0025 of a second longer than a day in Fall; this variation is attributed to the movement of great masses of the atmosphere about the globe as the seasons change. The third kind of variation in the Earth's rate of spin falls under a catch-all phrase—'irregular fluctuations', which means anything that the earth scientists and astronomers cannot explain by the first two effects. This looks like the sort of place where we might find a trigger for unusual earthquake activity, since the strain caused by a changing spin of the Earth must be dissipated somewhere. But there is a lot to be learned about the overall behavior of the Earth from a quick look at the first two kinds of variation as well.

It is worth a slight detour from our main trail to see how astronomers have been able to measure the slow, steady increase in the length of day from historic records, even without such modern aids as atomic clocks. Working at the Johns Hopkins University in Maryland,

Dr. R. R. Newton (a happy name for an astronomer) has investigated astronomical records left by a great scholar who lived about 1000 years ago and rejoiced in the name Abu al-Raihan Muhammad bin Ahmed al-Biruni. Al-Biruni seems to have had an adventurous life; born in 973 AD, he was involved in civil war, became a friend of princes, and was taken hostage in 1017 by Sultan Mahmud of Ghazni. He remained in the realm of the Sultan who had made him a hostage for the rest of his life, although we can take it that this did not involve any unusual hardship for the times in which he lived. He wrote many books, several of which survive intact to this day. One in particular contains information which enabled Dr. Newton to work out the rate at which the Earth's length of day was changing around 1000 AD.

According to al-Biruni, this book was intended to determine the direction of the great circle from Ghazni to Mecca in order that the devotee might face in the correct direction at the proper times. Apparently this was a standard justification used by Islamic astronomers to obtain official approval for their fundamental research. In this respect they probably differ little from scientists involved in fundamental research today, who must find some mundane justification for their work before it receives the approval of the committees which disperse the money. Because the coordinates of Baghdad relative to Mecca were already known, al-Biruni calculated the coordinates of Ghazni relative to Baghdad. In so doing he used, among other methods, observations of the elevation of the Sun to determine latitudes. Knowing latitudes exactly, and measuring distances along the ground, he had enough information to calculate longitudes. Fortunately for modern astronomers, al-Biruni often gave the original observations of the Sun—the 'raw data' from which other information can be obtained by different calculations. In addition he quotes measurements of the time of the autumnal equinox which go back to Hipparchus in 161 BC—further from al-Biruni in time than al-Biruni is from us. The equinoxes are the times of equal day and equal night, when the Sun seems to cross the celestial equator from south to north (Spring) or north to south (Fall). So the legacy of his writings represents something of a gold mine to astronomers today who want to know how the Earth and the Solar System have changed during historic time.

But modern astronomers have not had all their work done for them, since first they must identify all the observations recorded by ancients such as al-Biruni (eclipses and so on) with events they know must have happened. This is done by calculating the movements of the Sun, Moon and Earth in a computer, and running the model backwards. Even then the calculation of such a small effect as the steady change in the Earth's spin requires painstakingly accurate work. Fascinating though the investigation into the work of al-Biruni and similar scholars is, we can be thankful that our interest in the Earth's spin is from the point of view of related earthquake effects. Thus we can concentrate on the most recent studies where the atomic clock makes direct measurement of time changes possible. Dr. R. A. Challinor, of the University of Toronto, has gathered evidence of all three kinds of change which we mentioned earlier, covering the decade and a half from 1955 to 1970.

Like the study of the polar wobble, trying to sort out what is happening to the rate at which the Earth is spinning means sorting out many effects which are made manifest in a similar fashion. Like the Russian dolls which fit one inside the other, each discovery about the Earth's motion is hidden inside a large effect. Dr. Challinor sorted out the larger effects, putting them aside so that the smaller, more detailed variations would be revealed. First of all the precession and Chandler Wobble of the Earth must be discounted. This is no great problem because astronomical observations provide a standard of time in which the effects of these motions have been allowed for. This is called Universal Time One (UT1): basic universal time (UT0) is calculated with the wobble effects left in, and this is the time used by navigators and astronomers —it is essentially the same as Greenwich Mean Time. Using atomic clocks, available since 1955, there is an independent standard of time called atomic time (AT). Since the mid-1950s the staff of the United States Naval Observatory have kept daily records of the difference between AT and UT0, which are based on measurements of the transit of thirty stars above each of two observing stations on every night of the year. It is a simple matter to work out the corresponding values of AT–UT1 from these measurements. Because the Earth is slowing down in its spin rate over the centuries, the day is now slightly longer than twenty-four hours; that is, the difference between AT and UT1 is slowly increasing on average. But as we have already seen, over one year the spin of the Earth both increases and decreases. From these daily observations Dr. Challinor has taken averages over each month from the beginning of 1956 to the end of 1969. These show the steady, long-term change in the length of day (the mean yearly length of day is simply given by averaging twelve monthly means) as well as seasonal variations, and the ragbag of other effects (see figure 10).

The next problem is to get rid of the seasonal vari-

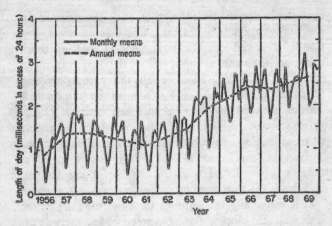

FIGURE 10. Variations in the length of day, derived from
AT—UT1, for the years 1956–1969.

ations. What Dr. Challinor has done is to use a 'harmonic analysis' to find out exactly how the pattern of one year's variations in the length of day repeats in the next and subsequent years. The speeding up of the Earth between Spring and Fall is very clear (see figure 10) but how many of the other wiggles in the graph are the result of seasonal effects? It seems that there are three long-term secular and periodic effects. As well as the strictly yearly variation there are six-month and four-month variations—harmonics corresponding to one-half and one-third of the main twelve-month variation like the harmonics of musical notes. At last it looks as if we are getting somewhere. If all the periodic variations have been removed, then anything which is left is by definition erratic effects.

We are not quite out of the woods however, because Dr. Challinor is not the only person who has looked in detail at variations in the length of day. There are,

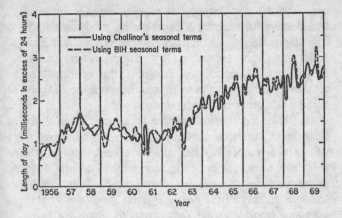

FIGURE 11. Variations in the length of day, after removal of the first two seasonal terms, for the years 1956–1969.

in particular, some distinct differences between the exact values for the seasonal variations which Dr. Challinor has calculated and the equivalent values which are circulated by the Bureau Internationale de l'Heure (BIH). These differences do not affect the overall pattern of variations in the length of day, and we can certainly take Challinor's results as a good indication of the way the Earth behaves. What we cannot say, until years of more patient observation are completed, is that Challinor's results are *exactly* right. But since the differences we are talking about amount to only a few thousandths of a second (a few milliseconds) in a day twenty-four hours long, they will not affect any general conclusions which are made. Some idea of the really very good agreement between Challinor's calculations and those of the BIH is given in figure 11. Both sets of measurements are plotted with the yearly and six-monthly parts of the seasonal variation taken out. The BIH version of this plot defines the international standard time UT2. Most people who have studied this variation are convinced that the annual seasonal variations are caused by the movement of the atmosphere. What of the irregular fluctuations—the remaining wiggles in figure 11 which stop the plot from being a smoothly increasing line?

Challinor has pointed out that the amplitude of these irregular fluctuations depends on just how the seasonal effects are removed. After all, he argues, it is just a matter of taste, not scientific fact, which has produced the difference between his plot and the BIH graph. Could it be that all the irregular fluctuations are merely leftovers from seasonal factors which have not been properly estimated? It is even possible to make out a case of that these irregular variations are due partly to small inaccuracies in the measurements. We are talking, after all, about fractions of a millisecond—but this is unlikely to cause all the wiggles in figure 11. Dr. G. Rochester has pointed out that these irregular changes in the Earth's rotation, which amount to a substantial fraction of a millisecond over a few days or weeks, produce physically important *accelerations* as great as those noted by Dr. Donald Anderson over the decade between 1900 and 1914. These accelerations are proportioned to the rotational torques and they tell us something about the stress within the crust. It is through the work of Drs. D. Pines and J. Shaham that we learn of a large source of elastic energy, which these irregular accelerations, either of a short term or over a solar cycle, may draw upon to trigger earthquakes. The use of laser ranging of the Moon and very long base line interferometry will enable time intervals of these abrupt accelerations to be narrowed down to a fraction of a day, so that they may be correlated with

improved global meteorological data. Thus the simplest explanation seems to be that the irregular variations are caused by fluctuations in the movement of
the atmosphere, which are related to the seasonal variations but do not follow exactly the same pattern
every year. If the circulation of the atmosphere did
follow exactly the same pattern every year, we would
have no need of weather forecasters; our everyday
experience provides a good clue to the detailed un-
predictability of air movements, even if we can be sure
of the order of the seasons.

The Influence of the Solar Wind on the Atmosphere of the Earth

What is the nature of these irregular fluctuations in
the Earth's atmosphere and what causes them? Observations of weather patterns points to a causal effect
linking the activity of the Sun and the occurrence of
large atmospheric low-pressure troughs crossing the
region of the Gulf of Alaska and the Aleutian Islands.
Norman Macdonald and Walter Roberts, of the University of Colorado, have studied weather patterns in
the Alaska-Aleutians area, and also the geomagnetic
disturbances of the Earth's ionosphere by the high energy particles emitted from the Sun. These cosmic rays
are produced in solar flares during times of sunspot
activity. Upon reaching the Earth they interact with
the Earth's magnetic field to produce aurorae and magnetic storms which affect radio communications; later
in the book we will look more closely at what happens
on the Sun to produce these effects, and at how the
solar cosmic ray particles and other products of the
solar activity are transmitted across space to interact
with the Earth and its atmosphere. But just now we are

chiefly interested in what goes on when the cosmic rays from the Sun reach the Earth's magnetosphere.

People were aware of the Earth's magnetic field before it was known that the Earth is round. Ancient Chinese and mongul travelers made use of the curious property possessed by lode stones of always pointing to a fixed direction on the Earth's surface. This point lies close to the North Pole, which is why the Pole Star is also known as the Lode Star. In the southern hemisphere the Earth has another, opposite pole, rather like a bar magnet. We have already mentioned in the discussion on the magnetic tape recorder in chapter 1 how these poles can switch unpredictably; this is something a bar magnet cannot do, and may be a result of the way in which the Earth's magnetism is generated. The fluid core of our planet is swirled around by its spin. The magnetic lines of force produced by the terrestrial dynamo emerge from the poles, curving out into space, leveling out above the equator and then dipping back down to the other pole. Just now the North Pole is at 76°N 100°W and the South Pole is at 66°S 139°E—not quite at the geographic poles. Both magnetic poles wander slightly relative to the Earth's spin axis, as well as indulging in the switching behaviour which geophysicists have found so useful in their studies of fossil magnetism.

Soon after the dawn of the space age the American physicist James van Allen discovered the belts of charged particles about 1000 km above the Earth's surface. These atoms in the tenuous outer fringe of the atmosphere are stripped of their electrons to produce charged positive ions; both electrons and ions are then trapped by the Earth's magnetic field. The charged particles funnel down towards the magnetic poles by spiraling around magnetic lines of force, and produce the spectacular aurorae by exactly the same process as the lighting of neon tubes. The glow of a neon tube has the characteristic color of charged neon ions; in the same way the different colors green, blue, white and red of aurorae can each be identified with a different ion, including those of oxygen, nitrogen and sodium. At times of sunspot maximum, the aurorae cover wide zones around both poles and reach heights from 80 to 320 km above the ground. They can be observed from almost anywhere above about 50 degrees latitude, and the patterns seen—rays, vaguely intertwined glows and curtains of light-change quickly. It now seems that they also change the weather patterns in the atmosphere below.

Aurorae and the Weather

Macdonald and Roberts define 'key days' for the effect of the solar particles on the Earth's atmosphere. These are either days on which a sudden magnetic storm began (revealed by its effect on radio reception) or the day on which a strong auroral display began, as reported independently by the University of Saskatchewan. Both of these effects result from the sudden arrival of bursts of solar particles at the Earth's atmosphere; as yet we will not worry about how or why the particles were emitted from the Sun. As far as weather patterns were concerned, the Colorado team asked meteorologists who did not know about the timing of auroral activity to select the days on which troughs of low pressure either formed or moved into the Alaska–Aleutian area. Then they compared the times for the two sets of observations. After the critical 'key days' there are a greater number of deep troughs and correspondingly fewer minor troughs. According to

Macdonald and Roberts the odds against this being a coincidence are 100 to 1. Only troughs which appear between two and four days after the 'key days' show this affect, and the only logical conclusion seems to be that the particles from the Sun are causing a deepening in some of the shallow troughs. During the years of minimum solar activity the statistical significance of these results fell somewhat; however, there is strong evidence of a preferential enhancement of vorticity over the Gulf of Alaska two to four days after auroral activity. This preferential enhancement of winds in the polar regions over equatorial regions will, as we shall see, be enough to cause significant irregular variations in the length of day.

This discovery raises many interesting questions; apart from anything else, the energy contained in large-scale wind motions comprising the low-pressure troughs below about 15 km altitude is far greater than the energy of the solar particles arriving at the upper atmosphere, or stratosphere, 50 km above the ground and at least 35 km above the weather patterns being affected. Possibly the input of energy high in the stratosphere from solar particles decreases the temperature gradient there, and energy which normally conducts upwards from the troposphere is deflected into horizontal motions (low-pressure troughs) by this 'lid' that is placed on the lower boundary of the upper atmosphere. Somehow increases in solar activity, as indicated by changes in the magnetosphere of the Earth and in particular by auroral displays, provide a reliable indicator of imminent changes in the weather patterns of the Earth at high latitudes. Late in 1973 work done by Dr. J. King, of the Appleton Laboratory, tied changes in weather in the northern hemisphere even more firmly to changes in the Suns output of cosmic rays over several of the eleven-year solar cycles of sunspot activity.

Late in 1974, two Czech physicists, Drs. A. Zatopek and L. Křivský demonstrated that streams of active solar particles and fields affect not only the upper layers of the Earth's atmosphere near the polar cap, but shook the ground itself via the motions of a complex circumpolar atmospheric phenomena known as "the great polar vortex." The relation between the shaking of the solid earth meteorological microseisms, i.e. quasi-harmonic oscillations of the Earth's surface (period range 3 to 10 seconds) due to atmospheric pressure variations at the ocean's bottom, and circulation of the polar vortex is well understood. However, these two Czech physicists also demonstrate that there is an additional close relationship between solar phenomena over an entire 11-year cycle and the microseisms, as shown by the seismic instruments, (negative) intensity variations of cosmic rays and the occurrence of solar flares associated with type IV radio emissions from the Sun. The importance of these observations is that they relate solar activity to longer-term, worldwide climatological phenomena.

The Weather and Changes in the Length of Day

Physically, changes in the length of day are linked to stresses that arise from wind shear at the surface of the Earth, and a slight excess in the pressure on the windward side over the lee side of obstacles like mountains and waves. The magnitude of wind stress at the surface of the Earth is larger by a factor of one hundred than the minimum values required to account for the observed variation in the length of day. Suppose the winds over the Arctic mountains were to increase suddenly due to solar disturbance of wind patterns. There would be an immediate and pronounced effect on the length of day, but its persistence is limited to a few weeks at most. The effect of high-frequency variations in the length of day may be of the same order as the annual term. A weakening of the west winds and a poleward shift of air mass would, by itself, decrease the length of day; this is precisely the effect suggested by Roberts.

In our search for phenomena related to a trigger for earthquake activity we have looked for the source of irregular changes in the Earth as it spins through space. The evidence points towards irregular changes in the atmosphere, since the outermost part of the Earth is spinning at faster speeds than regions nearer to the axis of rotation. These changes affect the total spin of the whole Earth system and might help to trigger incipient earthquakes in regions where tension has built up. Seasonal variations in the atmosphere, caused by regular changes in the heating of the Earth as it moves around the sun in an elliptical orbit, cause long-term, secular, regular changes in the spin rate of the Earth and in the length of day. Some unknown effect linked with solar activity may disturb atmospheric circulation and cause it to produce irregular changes in the Earth's spin rate. Obviously, to find other effects which can change the regular behaviour itself from time to time we must look outside the Earth. Can other solar effects provide irregular disturbances of the atmosphere? Or might some other effect in the Solar System disturb the Earth's spin? Both possibilities seem promising in the light of the growing wealth of information which astronomers are gaining about the Sun and the Solar System, much of this information coming from the Earth satellites and space probes which are now available.

6 Do Earth Tides Trigger Quakes?

We have seen how the changes in the spin rate of the Earth, which can be measured by comparing Universal Time and Atomic Time, are the result of a combination of several different processes. Basically, predictable long-term seasonal effects and the Chandler Wobble combine with shorter, irregular jerks. These effects are caused by tidal forces of the Sun and Moon and by movements of great air masses over the oceans and continents following the pattern of warming and cooling of the seasons. The tidal forces, of course, raise and lower the levels of the oceans; these regular motions of water, passing in some places through narrow inland seas and estuaries, inevitably result in a loss of energy through friction. Similarly, movements of air masses cause energy and momentum to be lost by the planet Earth, and this is why the spin of our planet is affected.

But what of the solid Earth itself? The tides in the oceans are obvious to anyone who has lived by the sea for more than a day, and we have all felt the winds in the atmosphere associated with movements of air masses. Few people, however, realize that the land also experiences tidal effects—the ground moves by as much as 10 cm up and down over a twelve-hour period. These earth tides are less dramatic than ocean tides— but then again friction plays a potent role in solids as well as liquids, so they provide a very important contribution to the energy losses of planet Earth and thus to changes in the spin rate. Earth tides arise both from the periodic tidal action of the Sun and Moon, and from changes in the Earth's spin due to variations in pressure over the land caused by the atmospheric movements. The tides cause some regions to be compressed and others to be stretched or placed in tension. When the Sun and the Moon are on the horizon, compression forces are greatest; thus quakes would be expected early in the morning or late in the afternoon. Conversely, for fault zones under tension, tidal forces are most important when the Sun and Moon are overhead.

The next step in the chain is not very well understood as yet, but the idea we are now going to follow up is that these forces, either separately or in a combination, can act to trigger the titanic forces stored up in areas of danger like the locked portions of the San Andreas Fault. Just as a tiny push can send a boulder over the edge of a cliff, releasing its potential energy in a destructive fashion, so the potential energy stored in the stretched rocks of the San Andreas Fault might be released by a relatively small trigger. In Chapter 4 we saw how a stress applied to rocks over periods of hours or days helps to bring them ever closer to breaking point. Tidal forces apply just this kind of pressure over just the right sort of time scales. Even more important, as we shall find from a closer look at earth tides, the energy dissipated in them is focused chiefly at the margins of continental tectonic plates and in regions where seafloor spreading is of the greatest importance. Few areas in the world fit this description better than the San Andreas–Baja California region. Even though the effects of earth tides are small for the

Earth as a whole, they are concentrated in just those regions of our planet which are most likely to be triggered into more violent activity.

The Nature of Earth Tides

But perhaps we are racing ahead too fast in our pursuit of the ultimate cause of the earthquakes so typical of California. What exactly are these earth tides, and how do geophysicists set about measuring them? The force of gravity acts upon every piece of the Earth, pulling it towards the center, but the solid part of the Earth exerts an outward hydrostatic force which partly cancels out the force of gravity. However, the direction of the downward force of gravity is not quite the same as the outward pressure. There remains a small residual force which creates *horizontal* displacements along the Earth's surface; it is this tidal force that causes the familiar masses of water to surge around the Earth. The exact size and direction of the force we feel on our bodies depends on whereabouts we are on the Earth— we would weigh slightly more at the poles than at the equator. The story is further complicated by the pull of the Sun and the Moon. On its own the spinning Earth rapidly would settle down as a more or less uniform sphere rather fatter around the equator than around a circle passing through both poles. But because the pull of the Sun and the Moon depends on their exact distances from the Earth, and these distances vary, each particle in the solid part of the Earth (and for that matter, in the Sun and the Moon as well) feels a varying total force which is at any instant the sum of gravity pull of the Earth, the Moon and the Sun, and the hydrostatic force plus the centripetal force of the spinning Earth. So the whole Earth is contantly flexing in an attempt to adjust to the changing balance of forces. Earth tides and oceanic tides are usually divided into daily (diurnal), half-daily (semi-diurnal) and longer period tides. Irregular tides caused by shifts in air masses cannot be so neatly classified, since they have no fixed pattern of motion.

Geophysicists use sensitive instruments to measure the deviation of local 'gravity' at different points from a geometrical straight line to the center of the Earth, and they also monitor the changing strength of the force. Tiltmeters, gravity-tide meters and strain meters are among the battery of instruments used in these studies. Just as astronomers divide Universal Time up into different components which represent different features of the Earth's changing spin, so geophysicists divide the force of gravity, represented by g, up into different components. g_1 is the force which an object would feel on the surface of a completely rigid undeformable Earth; g_2 represents the effects felt on a completely symmetrical and oceanless but otherwise realistic Earth; g_3 is the varying contribution produced by the moving oceans and tides; and g_4 is a 'grab bag' into which all other effects are put—for example, local effects caused by the elasticity of rocks in a particular area, and whether or not nearby dense ore deposits are present. These geophysical instruments measure local irregularities and changes caused by the changing tidal forces just as measures of AT–UT monitor changes in the Earth's spin rate. Changes in the stress caused by tides should be traceable across whole continents, but they are not at present because of a lack of geophysical stations. This kind of wave of stress within the Earth is the sort of process which we expect to unleash the locked regions of the San Andreas Fault once strain in the fault is built up to a critical value.

Earth Tides, Heat Flow and Plate Tectonics

So tidal forces introduce a number of irregular and cyclical stresses in the Earth. These stresses are small compared with the tectonic forces which shape the ever-changing face of the globe, but some are periodic, and they are rapid. Further, Dr. Herbert Shaw of the United States Geological Survey has recently shown that the power of earth tides concentrates along the ocean ridges, where new seafloor is created, and at the plate boundaries, where the pieces of the great worldwide jigsaw puzzle jostle against one another. The tidal energy can be converted into heat and volcanic activity in these regions (see figure 1, page 4) where sideways (lateral) motions produce shear zones and pieces of the Earth's crust rub together as the wave of tidally-induced stress passes. The San Andreas Fault system described in chapters 1 and 2 is an ideal example of a region where these effects come into play.

Earthquake activity is a powerful process for dissipating mechanical energy from earth tides and other causes of strain. Periodic changes in stress caused by lunar or solar tides, or sudden, irregular changes in the rotation rate of the Earth due to solar activity and the large-scale movements of air masses, can generate this strain which is then dissipated in the margins of tectonic plates. These effects do not *drive* the earthquakes —indeed, the energy involved in these particular strains represents only a small percentage of the flow of heat from the Earth's interior which maintains the seafloor spreading. But the concentration of oceanic tidal dissipation in a few shallow seas shows how the dissipation involved in earth tides could concentrate the worldwide tidal energy in a few favored locations—the regions we know to be plate margins. In the west of

North America, as we have seen, the continent has overridden a 'mid-ocean' ridge. So the activity of the region is in many ways like the tectonic activity of ocean ridges—a combination of slip-stick motion and the remnant of the heat source rifting Baja California by thermal convection. This is an ideal system for the concentration of dissipative tidal forces.

Moonquakes Triggered by Tides

Perhaps the best evidence of the way which quakes can be triggered by earth tides comes from the Moon. There, where there is no atmosphere and no oceans, the only tides are the solid tides induced by the Earth and the Sun. Now that the Apollo missions have established a chain of automatic seismic stations across the Moon, moonquake activity can be monitored continuously. This monitoring shows clearly that most moonquakes occur at perigree and apogee, when the strain associated with solid tides caused by the Earth's gravity is greatest.

In a recent report prepared for NASA by Dr. G. Lathan and colleagues, the evidence is gathered to show how, around the time of perigree, 80 per cent of the moonquake activity occurs in a zone 800 km below the moon's surface, consistent with the idea that internal strain is being released. There is some evidence that similar tidal stresses trigger earthquakes—but of course the Earth is so large relative to the Moon that the effect of the Moon on earthquakes is much harder to detect than the effect of the Earth on moonquakes, since quakes on the Moon and Earth duffer by a factor of 10^{13} in energy release. Careful statistical analysis of large masses of earthquake data shows that the effect does occur but it is not of overwhelming importance in itself. What is of the greatest importance, however, is that this work provides firm confirmation that earthquakes can be triggered by events occurring outside the Earth. If the small, regular earth tides caused by the Moon's gravity can, by concentrating dissipative energy at plate margins, act to trigger earthquakes, then there can be little doubt that events large enough to produce sudden, marked changes in the Earth's spin will do the same on a larger scale. The possibility of this type of seismic activity on the Earth being triggered by tidal stresses has not been ignored; indeed there exists direct evidence of tidal triggering in a volcanic region in Alaska, in the Galapagos and in other seismically active regions in the USA and USSR.

Nevada Earthquakes

It has taken a geophysicist from the Azerbaidzhan Republic in the USSR, Dr. G. P. Tamrazyan, to develop the proper statistical tools to show that earthquakes are related to tidal phenomena. Since moonquakes are related to maximum stress, it seemed reasonable to use the exactly known periods of lunar and solar motion to 'tune' into a large compilation of earthquake data to look for unusual patterns. This 'heterodynning' technique is useful for rooting out information (for example whether earthquakes are triggered preferentially at perigee and new or full Moon) from the 'noise' that random changes in stress patterns, geology and so on can make in different seismic regions. Tamrazyan has shown when earthquakes were linked to lunar phase (that is the tidal influence of the Moon) and to eccentricities in the lunar orbit, a remarkable change occurs in the statistics. Within a few days after the Moon's passage through perigee the number of earthquakes in Nevada increased by 800 per cent.

Volcanic Seismicity in the Galapagos

An even more dramatic and direct proof of the power of the tides to trigger earthquakes was made recently by Dr. T. Simkin of the Museum of Natural History in Washington, D.C. Dr. Simkin and others went to the Galapagos Islands in 1968 to study volcanoes in this area associated with tectonic plates. He was extremely fortunate to witness a rare geologic event of the collapse of a large volcanic caldera. Early in the sequence of eruptions the earthquakes associated with the collapse of the caldera showed a six-hour period. As can be seen in figure 12, earthquakes coincided with extrema in the semi-diurnal type of earth tides actually measured on the Galapagos. Indeed, for the first period of forty-two hours earthquakes occurred *only* at each and every extremium of the local ocean tide. Also shown in figure 12 is a fortnightly tidal maximum which occurred on the night of 11 June 1968; at the exact time when a large explosive eruption began the caldera collapse, the moon was a perigee and the solar tidal force was at its maximum.

Dr. Simkin found that the release of seismic energy occurred when the volcano was under maximum horizontal tension and vertical compression from the tidal forces of the Sun and Moon. These tidal forces may act to release energy by forcing fluids (either water or magma) through the pores of the rocks under stress, thus seriously reducing their strength. (We have seen in chapter 4 that when water was poured into oil wells numerous earthquakes resulted). At shallow depths it may be that variable artesian pressure acts to weaken rocks under stress, while deep-focus earthquakes may be triggered off by variable tidal forces pumping the liquid magma into the heated rocks.

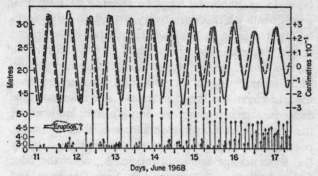

FIGURE 12. This graph shows the correlation of earthquakes with the phase of the ocean and earth tides during the period 11–17 June 1968. The solid line represents the high and low ocean tide recorded at Baltra Island in the Galapagos. The scale is given on the left in meters with respect to mean low water. The dashed line represents the radial component of the earth tide computed for the Galapagos at the approximate time. The scale of this bodily tide, given on the right ordinate, is in tens of centimeters of water above an equilibrium level on an ideal, rigid earth. The arrows mark the time of occurrence of earthquakes. The length of these arrows indicates the strength of the earthquake (scale on the lower left).

We have already seen in Chapter 5 the maxima in the number of aurorae in the sunspot cycle and the mean length of day are linked by irregular movements of the atmosphere. It also seems likely that one can also relate solar activity to the triggering of earthquakes by irregular earth tides. These conditions, however, are also fulfilled by lunar and solar gravitational forces; which type of tidal force predominates at any given time to trigger earthquakes depends on a number of unknown and probably unknowable circumstances. As R. A. Corradini and N. N. Parryski and other Russian geophysicists have pointed out, one must consider more than the gravitational component of the earth

tides. More important may be the several tangential
components which depend very strongly on the orien-
tation of a fault in a region. In general, the extremes
in the tangential tidal components do not occur at the
time of the extremes of the gravitational component.
Thus several studies of tides and earthquakes have
tried to cover too large an area. Since tides are time
dependent and periodic in nature, considerations of
large regions have averaging effects on their variation,
possibly masking the real effects and giving statistics
that show no significance of relationships between tides
and earthquakes. It is clear that both Challinor and
Tamrazyan have related earthquakes to different sorts
of tidal energies, both of which are dissipated in the
margins of the tectonic plates. We shall now go on to
show how specific changes in the Earth's rotation can
be related to very large bursts of particles and radiation from the Sun.

7 How Solar Flares and Cosmic Rays Affect the Earth's Spin

In 1956 the average length of day was one millisecond greater than twenty-four hours; in 1971, fifteen years later, the average length of day was twenty-four hours and three milliseconds. But within both of those years —and all the years in between—the Earth's spin was both accelerated and decelerated by the many variations discussed earlier. Just like crashing in a car or plane, it is the suddenness of the acceleration (or deceleration) in the Earth's spin which is likely to do the damage as far as the Earth's spin and consequent tidal forces triggering earthquakes is concerned. In the early 1950s some astronomers suggested that there seemed to be a sudden change in the acceleration of the Earth's spin roughly every ten years or so. Could this be tied to the familiar solar sunspot cycle, which has a period close to eleven years?

Challinor has compared the annual mean rate of change of the length of day with the annual mean number of sunspots and with the occurrence of earthquakes greater than magnitude 7·5 for the years from 1957 to 1968—one complete sunspot cycle. He found a very clear suggestion of a relationship between the changing length of day and the sunspot number (see figure 13). Quite simply, changes in the Sun's activity (shown by changes in the numbers of sunspots) are related to the Earth's spin. Challinor also notes a 'slight correlation' between the rate of general earthquake activity—that is, the number of large earthquakes occurring in a year

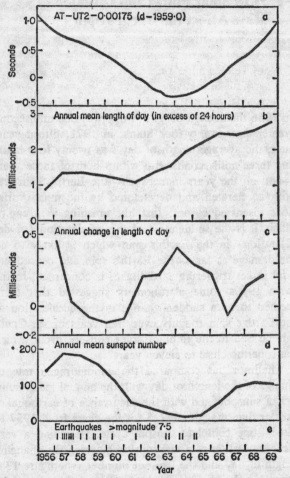

FIGURE 13. Comparison of annual mean rate of change of length of day with annual mean number of sunspots and with earthquakes greater than magnitude 7·5.

—and the annual change in length of day. He is very doubtful about the reality of all these possible links, partly because, as he puts it, 'to surmise that all of these exist . . . would, among other things, suggest a relationship between earthquakes and solar activity'. But that is just the sort of relationship that we are looking for.

Many studies have looked for links in the sense that the earthquake activity might cause wobble in the Earth's axis, but it would be ridiculous to suggest that a further link could be built in that direction and that such changes in the Earth might affect the Sun. Surely, though, in the opposite direction, the links between the Earth and the Sun are not only possible but probable. Solar influence on atmospheric circulation is inevitable and the atmosphere can, it seems, affect both the Earth's spin and possibly the incidence of earthquakes. Seasonal heating of the atmosphere clearly accounts for some of these changes, but the Earth receives much more from the Sun than just heat and light. The solar wind and the interplanetary magnetic field of the Solar System provide further links between the Sun's activity and the spin of the Earth. The trail we are following begins to look very warm indeed.

If the average changes in the eleven-year sunspot cycle cause gradual changes in the rate at which the length of day is changing, might not sudden, unusual sunspot activity produce instantaneous effect on the Earth? In 1959 a great and unusual 'storm' occurred on the Sun when, on 15 July, there was a very large solar flare. There was advanced a claim (dismissed at that time by most people) concerning a sudden, corresponding change in the rotation of the Earth. Unfortunately 1959 was a little too early for this gigantic flare to be monitored by the new generation of space vehicles which now operate above the Earth's atmo-

sphere, which screens out so many of the effects of the
Sun's activity. In 1972, however, astronomers were
more fortunate when an even greater flare occurred on
the Sun. This time a whole battery of space equipment
was available with which this dramatic event could be
studied.

The Great Solar Flares of July 1959 and August 1972

Activity on the Sun is measured by the number of sunspots visible on the solar disc. These complex sunspot
groups show alternate cycles of activity and relative
calm within a period of about eleven years. The sunspot groups themselves are caused by, and outline the
region of influence of, areas on the Sun in which the
solar magnetic field is unusually strong—as much as
several thousand gauss. (The Earth's magnetic field, by
comparison, is about $0 \cdot 6$ gauss at the magnetic poles
and $0 \cdot 3$ gauss at the equator; $1 \text{ gauss} = 10^{-4}$ tesla.)
Solar flares, which can produce dramatic effects in the
polar regions of the Earth, occur within sunspot groups
and produce floods of solar cosmic ray particles, radio
waves, X-rays and brilliant white light. Just how the
particles are emitted is not understood, but they emerge
from the Sun at relativistic velocities, that is, velocities
very close to the speed of light, so that their mass increases due to the effects which are explained by Ein-
tein's special theory of relativity.

Early August 1972 witnessed two of the greatest
solar flares ever. Only in July 1959 has anything similar been recorded, and that flare in turn occurred at a
time when the overall activity of the Sun was more
pronounced than at any time since 1610, when Galileo
first recorded the existence of sunspots. The great 1972

solar flare is even more remarkable since it occurred at a time when the Sun was, on the whole, unusually quiet. It came almost literally 'out of the blue', and was totally unexpected by astronomers. Of the many spacecraft that were in orbit in the summer of 1972, some, like Pioneer 10, were on long missions to the depths of space, while others were performing routine observations of the Sun and space near the Earth. OSO–7, for example, carried instruments which operate at the frequencies of gamma rays, which are extremely energetic bursts of electromagnetic radiation. Both satellites recorded the two August flares, and the observed radiation bore the characteristic spectral signature of elements such as carbon and oxygen—elements already known to exist in the Sun, but observed for the first time at gamma ray frequencies. But we shall not dwell on these facts since we are particularly interested in the changes in the solar wind, which in turn can affect conditions on Earth.

Interplanetary space is filled by a plasma—a gas in which electrons have been stripped off the atoms, leaving charged ions—which moves outwards from the Sun with an average motion of about 400 km per second. Because the plasma is made up of charged particles it is a very strong conductor of solar electricity and magnetism. The solar lines of magnetic force are stretched outward, like elastic bands, as the solar wind blows away from the Sun. Cosmic rays from outside the Solar System are also electrically charged, and when they run into this stretched solar magnetic field a lot of them fail to penetrate into the Solar System. When the great solar flares occurred, the speed of the solar wind jumped more than twice its normal speed, some 1100 km per second. Such an increase in speed also increased the effectiveness of the interaction between the plasma and the Sun's magnetic fields; and it produced an increase in the screening effect of the solar plasma against the background cosmic rays from outside the Solar System. Indeed, cosmic ray physicists find that ordinary solar flares and the associated increases in the solar wind sharply decrease the level of the background cosmic rays arriving at Earth from outside the Solar System. These rapid changes in the cosmic ray level are named Forbush decreases after their discoverer, and are usually followed by a more gradual return to a normal level of cosmic rays background. The event of August 1972 is different from this typical pattern behavior only in the degree of intensity of the effect.

The magnetic field pulled out from the Sun by the solar wind jumped by a factor or two when the rapidly moving plasma from the great August flare reached the satellite HEOS–2, in orbit around the Earth. This doubling of the magnetic field took it up to more than ten times the normal value recorded by HEOS–2 when the Sun is completely quiet, which is about sixty millionths of a gauss. The satellite Pioneer 10, on its lonely voyage to Jupiter and by then $3\frac{1}{2}$ times as far from the Sun as the Earth was, recorded this very noticeable jump in the solar wind speed and in magnetic field intensity. And at the same time, in the first of a series of Forbush decreases, the cosmic ray intensity near the Earth dropped to half the value it had before the storm.

During the July 1959 event the cosmic ray level measured at a polar station seven days after the flare, and after three Forbush decreases and three partial recoveries, was three-quarters of the level before the storm. In August 1972, however, the cosmic ray storm from out of the blue produced a slightly larger relative drop, by 27 per cent of the pre-storm intensity of cosmic rays after the first two Forbush decreases. And this, remember, when the Sun was supposedly in a 'quiet' period: In addition to the Forbush decreases, the cosmic ray intensity showed sharp increases—called Ground Level Events (GLEs) because they can be detected from the ground—which signal the arrival of the relativistic particles from the flares at the Earth. In figure 14 the observations made at a mid-latitude station during the 1972 flares are recorded graphically. The first Forbush decrease (FD1) is followed by a second decrease (FD2), a recovery and Ground Level Event, and by a third decrease. The later events are less spectacular, but show the continuing activity of the Sun associated with the second flare on 7 August.

The measurements made at the South Pole are very slightly more impressive than similar measurements made at other stations around the world. At 0130 (Universal Time) on 5 August, for instance, the intensity relative to the intensity before the storm was 72·5 per cent at Thule, 76·3 per cent at Swarthmore, 73·2 per cent at McMurdo Sound, and 66·8 per cent at the South Pole. The other three stations recorded much the same level of activity because they are all at sea level, beneath the same thick blanket of air, while South Pole Base is situated at an altitude of 3000 m, the height of the Antarctic plateau above sea level, and is much more thinly protected. Thule is in Greenland, Swarthmore in the equatorial regions, and McMurdo, like the South Pole, in Anarctica. So the truly worldwide significance of such cosmic ray storms can be seen easily in this example.

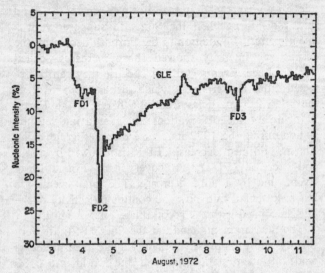

FIGURE 14. Observations of cosmic rays measured at a mid-latitude station on Earth during August, 1972. The pattern of Forbush decreases associated with the record-breaking solar activity can be clearly seen.

Effect of Interplanetary Processes on the Length of Day

With all the data available from space probes about the great solar flare of 1972, there is much clear, sound, scientific evidence about how such flares interacted with the Earth's magnetosphere. The science of space physics is far too young, of course, for anyone to be able to pinpoint exactly which solar processes will produce certain effects on the spin of the Earth and the changing length of day. But it does now seem that Dr. A. Danjon, of the Paris Observatory, might have been treated a little harshly when the scientific community dismissed, because of lack of evidence, his claim that the similar great solar flare of 1959 produced a sudden change in the length of day on Earth. Perhaps this is the time to rehabilitate some of Danjon's ideas, in the form in which they were elaborated by Dr. E. Schatzman in the mid-1960s.

Although the Sun emits cosmic rays, particularly during flares of at times of great sunspot activity, these are by no means the only energetic charged particles to reach the Earth from space. Many cosmic ray particles are produced elsewhere in our Galaxy, perhaps in the peculiar pulsating radio sources (pulsars) which have intrigued astronomers during the past few years, and it is even possible that some cosmic rays come from the distant regions of the Universe beyond our Galaxy. Whatever their origin, these particles flow continuously into our small Solar System, located in the outer regions of a rather insignificant galaxy which occupies no special position in the Universe. Paradoxically, when the Sun is active and pours great quantities of charged particles into interplanetary space, we see fewer cosmic rays on Earth—in other words, a Forbush decrease—because the enhanced solar wind acts as a shield against the cosmic rays from outside our Solar System. However, the cosmic ray astronomers term a sudden decrease in the number of cosmic rays reaching the surface of the Earth a 'storm', where in everyday terms it would be more appropriately called a lull. If the Sun's activity does affect the length of day, then surely it must be through the agency of the solar wind and the various effects of solar cosmic rays.

Now, Danjon's study of the events associated with the solar flare of 1959 was not just a few limited observations inspired by that remarkable event. He had been investigating possible relationships between the length of day and the cosmic ray activity seen on Earth for years before the 1959 disturbance came along, and he continued these studies for years afterwards. We saw earlier how Challinor related the length of day to sunspot number (see figure 13, page 82). When Danjon related the length of day to the flux of cosmic rays seen at the surface of the Earth, he was really doing exactly the same thing. We know from the cosmic ray and magnetic field detectors on board space vehicles that when there are more sunspots, there are less cosmic rays seen on Earth. In figure 15 the changing length of day is compared with the flux of cosmic rays from outside the Solar System reaching the Earth. The change in the length of day is calculated from the difference between Atomic Time (AT) and Universal Time 2 (UT2, the version of Universal Time with the Chandler Wobble and seasonal variations removed), and the graphs cover a continuous period from September 1960 to September 1961. This particular graph clearly shows the main effect which Danjon claimed to have discovered—that the length of day increases when there is a decrease in the number of cosmic rays reaching Earth; in other words, when the Sun is particularly active. In the graph we are recording the number of milliseconds by which UT2 lags behind AT, so a decrease in the difference simply means that UT2 is temporarily catching up with AT.

Scientists are—usually quite rightly—unwilling to accept evidence like this until it can be related in some way to the broad framework of their understanding of what makes the Universe tick. After all, one set of observations like those of Danjon could be a coincidence; in the life of the Earth and the Sun the paltry two decades of observations of cosmic rays is too short a period from which to draw general conclusions unless they can be embraced within a theoretical framework which explains many 'coincidences' of this kind. In addition to this understandable caution it must be said that scientists, like other people, are all too often afflicted with human prejudices. They are sometimes capable of dismissing even the most reliable piece of

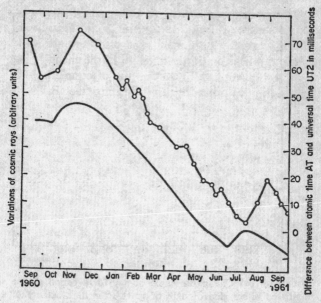

FIGURE 15. Variation of cosmic ray flux (lower curve) and the change in the length of day (upper curve) during 1960 and 1961.

evidence if it does not agree with their preconceived notions about what the world ought to be like. That is not to say that Danjon received an unfair deal ten years ago; if all new ideas are attacked in a friendly fashion and picked over for flaws then we can be fairly sure that the cranky ideas fall by the wayside and only good ideas, which better reflect the real nature of the world in some way, will stand up to the test of time. This is just what has happened to the idea that the Sun's activity influences the length of day.

After standing up to attack for so many years, the idea has reached a subtle stage of acceptance where most Earth and Solar System scientists no longer say

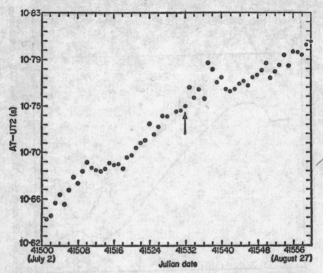

FIGURE 16. (a) Change in length of day for a period of one month on either side of date of great solar flare activity of August, 1972. Arrow marks August 3, the last day before the flare activity. Large discontinuous change in AT—UT2 occurs on 8 August.

that the evidence gathered is the result of inaccurate observations and coincidences, but instead conjecture, 'I wonder how such an interaction *could* work?'. It is this sort of enquiry which led Schatzman to turn up interesting historical evidence for a relationship which seems to be of such great importance to the stability of the Earth. For although cosmic rays have been detected only relatively recently, astronomers have been observing phenomena in the heavens with naked eye and telescope for centuries. How would these observations have been affected by solar activity and cosmic ray 'storms'? And can any such historical effect be related to changes in the length of day?

In this case the obvious thing to do, after Danjon reported the effect on the Earth's spin of the 1959 solar flare, was to wait for another such flare and look

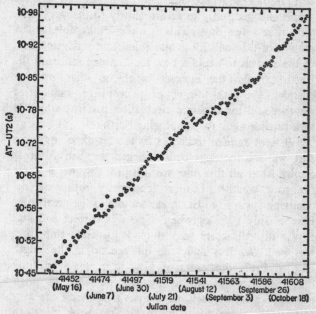

(b) May to October, 1972. The change in slope after the time of the great solar activity, and subsequent return towards the preflare slope, emphasize the importance of the event.

for a similar effect. We have been very lucky; although the 1959 flare was the largest for 350 years, there has already been an even more remarkable event, the great flare of August 1972 dicussed earlier (page 84).

Was there another sudden change in the length of day? We can certainly find very suggestive evidence in the form of measurements made by the United States Naval Observatory Time Service. Figure 16 shows the change in the Earth's spin, in the form AT–UT2, for a six-month period from May to October 1972. The solar flare reached its peak on 4 August; the arrow in the figure marks 3 August. Just after this there was a sudden jump in the record of AT–UT2 and the slope of the graph changed, only to return slowly to the usual pattern after a few days. This is quite remarkable confirmation of Danjon's ideas and Schatzman's development of these ideas to explain how the Sun can influence the Earth through the interaction of the solar wind of cosmic rays with the upper atmosphere, influencing weather and atmospheric circulation patterns which in turn provide a jolt to the spinning Earth.

What of *sudden* increases in the length of day, the sort we are looking for to trigger the San Andreas Fault? After all this time we will probably never know for sure whether Danjon incorrectly measured the changing spin of the Earth at the time of the great solar flare of July 1959 or whether he was correct and that it was his detractors who slipped up. The jump, if it was real, was less than one millisecond in the length of day. From our point of view it is also interesting that there was an above average incidence of small earthquakes (microseismic activity) just after the July 1959 solar event. On balance Danjon is aided by an impressive weight of circumstantial evidence in his favor. We are not concerned with proving a case in a court of law, but in working out an early warning system for great earthquakes (remember?); let us leave it that there is a strong case that unusual solar activity causes increased seismic activity by changing the Earth's rate of spin (or by triggering conditions which encourage these changes) and that there may have been such a sudden change at the time of the great solar flares of July 1959 and August 1972.

8 The Physical Links Between the Sun and the Earth

It is difficult to find a way in which the electromagnetic field of the Earth and the solar cosmic ray particles of the solar wind can interact directly to produce changes in the length of day. The Earth's magnetic field is generated in its liquid core, and it seems common sense that changes in the Earth's spin will be caused by the effect of charged particles from the Sun on the magnetic field of the Earth and hence on the core of the Earth. Evidence for this, however, is hard to find.

The Earth's Magnetic Field and Liquid Core

First of all, how does the liquid core interact through the mantle with the solid outer crust of the Earth? Below the thin outer crust, the mantle comprises 80 per cent of the Earth; it is highly unlikely that the part of the Earth inside the mantle is an exactly spherical cavity filled by some fluid which obeys the known viscosity equations exactly—but that situation is, unfortunately, about the only one concerning which any accurate behavioral predictions could be made. Still, some attempts have been made to get a handle on the problem. One possible system is provided by irregularities on the bottom of the solid outer layers; these upside-down mountains would drag through the sticky underlying fluid. However, seismic techniques cannot

tell us a great deal about the roughness of the under-
side of the crust, and we do not know just how sticky
(viscous) the interior fluid is. Estimates of the viscosity
differ from one another by a factor of more than ten
thousand million in extreme cases, which hardly makes
them of any practical use. The same sort of problems
crop up when anyone tries to estimate how the friction
between the smoother parts of the Earth's crust and
the viscous core fluid affects the spin of our planet;
surely it will be affected, but the numbers which come
out of any calculations are almost completely meaning-
less.

A slightly more promising line of attack is the study
of electromagnetic coupling between the inner and
outer parts of the Earth. The main magnetic field of the
Earth—the geomagnetic field—is just about the only
feature of the liquid core which can be studied in detail. The lower layers of the crust are also conductors
of electricity, and when an electrical conductor is in a
varying magnetic field there is a force on the conductor—this is the same force which drives an electric
motor. Once again, the properties of the real Earth do
not seem to be designed to make calculations easy, for
the geomagnetic field is not exactly a uniform dipole
field like that of a bar magnet; however it is still possible to get a fair idea of the degree to which the electrical currents induced in the conducting rocks of the
crust will bind the core and crust together, since
changes in the flow of electricity past the bottom of the
crust will produce an effect on the crust itself.

Because the core and the crust of the Earth are
slightly different in shape, the gravitational forces which
cause the polar motions discussed in chapter 5 are different for the two parts of the Earth system. Without
any form of coupling between them there would de-

velop very great differences between the rotational velocity of the outer parts of the core and the inner parts of the mantle. Thus the electromagnetic coupling probably plays a large part in ironing out differences which would tend to grow up over centuries or longer. Elementary calculations seem to rule out the possibility that electromagnetic coupling can play a part in the Chandler Wobble, let alone still more rapid variations than this fourteen-month recurrent pattern in the Earth's motion. As far as changes in the length of day are concerned, the electromagnetic coupling is good enough to account for about half a millisecond per decade but not quite enough to explain the most rapid fluctuations, unless geophysicists have calculated the electrical conductivity of the region just above the core incorrectly. That is possible, but it is even more probable that a combination of electromagnetic and viscous effects bind the two parts of the Earth together well enough for changes in the core at least to disturb the crust. Nevertheless we should look in this direction for an explanation of long-term irregular effects—not rapid fluctuations, which will be damped out all along the line by the 'stretch' of the geomagnetic field and by the viscosity of the core fluid.

The Solar-Magnetic Sector Structure and the Atmosphere

Over several hundred years, and with the aid of historical records, it is possible to get some idea of the longer period changes in the length of day, as was the case with al-Biruni's measurements and records. And of course, one clear pointer to the activity of the Sun is provided by the auroral displays seen at high latitudes. (In passing, it is worth recalling how much of a mystery the link between sunspots and aurorae must have been before cosmic rays were discovered!) According to Schatzman, the frequency of aurorae observed at latitudes south of 55°N in the northern hemisphere can be related to the average decrease in the length of day, from historical records going back to the turn of the seventeenth century. This remarkable piece of historical detective work can be linked to the other discoveries—more very large aurorae means more sunspots, and if anyone had been observing cosmic rays 200 years ago they would have found a corresponding decrease in the flux from outside our Solar System, as measured on Earth, at the time of bright aurorae.

And there is another clue—the sort of thing which does not stand up as a complete theory by itself but which in company with other evidence is very striking. It seems that the rate at which new comets are discovered over the years can be related to the eleven-year activity of the Sun. That, surely, should be dismissed as a coincidence—how could the number of comets depend on solar activity? It is just possible that increased solar activity excites comet tails when they are, on average, further out in the Solar System. Thus there is more time for smaller comets to be 'discovered' by astronomers. But as we have seen, the *weather* is affected by solar activity. Intense aurorae, caused by strong solar activity, presage the occurrence of deep low-pressure troughs with associated cloud systems and wet weather. And how can astronomers find new comets when the skies are cloudy? There is surely a moral here. The various pieces of evidence that the overall seismicity of the Earth is related to the solar activity perhaps falls into the same sort of category—sunspots need not cause earthquakes, but the processes which produce sunspots and solar flares may be linked to other processes which encourage earthquakes in the margins of the tectonic plates. Some steps in this process will take longer than others. The Sun seems to extend its influence out to the upper reaches of the Earth's atmosphere within hours; weather patterns are affected over periods of days following the arrival of the solar cosmic rays at the magnetosphere; and small-scale seismic activity may be enhanced for weeks as the atmosphere adjusts to a new balance of forces. How long will it take for the atmosphere to adjust to the effects of a great solar flare? And how long will it take for the solid Earth to react to large-scale changes in the atmospheric circulation? The interplanetary medium between the Earth and the Sun is dominated by a magnetic sector pattern which co-rotates with the Sun every twenty-seven days (see figure 17). One can envisage this phenomena of an interplanetary magnetic and particle field shaped in an Archimedian spiral or as the co-rotating grooves of a phonograph record. The needle slides along the grooves and moves nearly radially outward. The spiral interplanetary magnetic field is analogous to the grooves and the plasma sliding along the field lines is analogous to the phonograph needle. However, in the record the grooves control the motion of the needle, while in the interplanetary medium the solar-wind plasma is a hundred times stronger than the normal interplanetary magnetic field, so it is the radial motion of the plasma that stretches out the interplanetary field.

The solar wind speed and geomagnetic activity tend to rise to a peak in the preceding positive portion of the sector boundary and decline in the following negative portion. The cosmic rays, which initiate aurorae, seem to flow outward on one part of the sector bound-

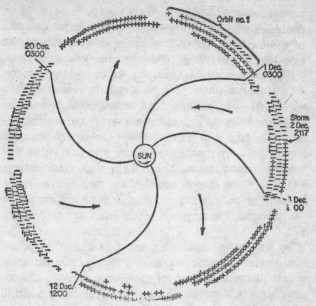

FIGURE 17. The plus signs (away from the Sun) and minus signs (toward the Sun) at the circumference of the figure indicate the direction of the measured interplanetary magnetic field during successive hour intervals. Parentheses around a plus or a minus sign indicate a time during which the field duration has moved beyond the 'allowed regions' for a few hours in a smooth and continuous manner. The inner portion of the figure is a schematic representation of a sector structure of the interplanetary magnetic field that is suggested by these observations. The deviations about the average streaming angle that are actually present are not shown.

ary and inward on the other (see figure 17). As this sector pattern rotates past the Earth, profound changes are observed in geomagnetic activity and the radiation belts. This increase in particle density near sector boundaries and the decline in the following portion correlates remarkably with certain weather phenomena.

Drs. John Wilcox and Walter Roberts at the National Center for Atmospheric Research in Boulder, Colorado, have shown that the solar magnetic sector structure appears to be related to the average area of low-pressure troughs observed in the winter of the northern hemisphere. The sectors have a width of 90 degrees in solar longitude, and although the boundaries of positive-negative polarity are very narrow the atmosphere begins to respond about two days before the sector boundary reaches the Earth. The physical mechanism initiating these changes is not made clear in their analysis; a clue may be found in the fact that there is a buildup of solar wind velocity and solar density on either side of the magnetic sector boundary (see figure 17).

So we are left with only one firm candidate as an intermediate stage in the transmission of sudden solar effects to the solid part of the Earth, namely, the atmosphere. Ridiculous though it might have seemed without the weight of evidence we have gathered, solar flares definitely cause a deepening of low pressure troughs—the Sun's activity causes extra-bad weather. There is certainly enough energy locked up in the atmosphere to drive variations in the Earth's spin (see chapter 6). Indeed it is from just this source that the energy which drives the seasonal variations comes. The atmosphere can play a key role in changing the length of day because it is on the outside of the spinning Earth, where angular momentum plays its biggest role. Effects which would be of little account in the core (spinning at the center of the Earth) become significant in these outer layers. And although there is still not enough energy in the solar particles themselves to change the Earth's spin noticeably, they would heat the upper atmosphere where they spiral down onto the poles. This local heating would encourage troughs to develop by drawing upon potential energy in the global weather system. If this is correct we have a series of triggers, a cascade process, from the solar activity down to the seismic activity. The next question is, what triggers the sunspot activity? We shall look into that in the next chapter, but first we can tidy up the picture by looking at how other small influences in the atmosphere of our planet (the solar and lunar tidal forces) can affect the weather.

Changes in the Solar Constant and the Weather

The possibility of variations in the solar "constant"—the amount of heat put out by the Sun—have often been invoked to explain some climatic changes. There have been many attempts to measure the solar constant (which climatologists prefer to call the solar "parameter") from the Earth, but such data collected from within the atmosphere must be contaminated by fluctuations in the turbidity of the air; no truly extraterrestrial study has yet been carried out, but high altitude balloon experiments have provided some interesting (and still controversial) results. One study of the solar parameter, by a Soviet group led by Kondratyev and Nikolsty, led to a suggestion that the parameter is related to sunspot number; this broadly agrees with a US study by Dr. R. Abbot, and suggests that as the sunspot number increases from zero the solar flux first increases (reaching a maximum 2 per cent greater than the zero sunspot value) but that after middling values of sunspot number are reached further increase in solar activity produces a decrease in solar parameter, which reaches its zero sunspot value again at peak solar activity, like that of 1958–1959.

These ideas have been incorporated in a climate model developed by Drs. S. Schneider and C. Mass, at the National Center for Atmospheric Research in Boulder, Colorado. They have used sunspot records to introduce solar parameter variations in line with the results of these experiments in modelling the climate of the past 200 years or so, and their model also takes account of known volcanic activity over the same period, which plays a part by throwing dust into the atmosphere and scattering some of the electromagnetic radiation from the Sun. Using the guesstimate that a 1 percent change in solar parameter corresponds to a change in mean surface temperature of about 0.65°C, Schneider and Mass are able to reproduce many features of recent climatic change, such as the 'Little Ice Age' peaking between 1650 and 1700; the cool spell at the beginning of the nineteenth century; the warming in the early part of the twentieth century; and the turndown of temperature since the middle of this century. Real extraterrestrial measures of the solar parameter are urgently needed to confirm or refute the accuracy of their assumptions about the link between temperatures and sunspot number; at present, the balance of evidence seems to be in favour of a genuine and useful discovery pointing to further links between the Sun and the Earth.

Lunar and Solar Tidal Influence on Terrestrial Weather

The regular oscillations of the atmosphere caused by the Sun and the Moon are called tides, even though they are partly attributable to the heating effect of the Sun. The atmospheric tides are numbered S_1, S_2 and so on for the solar tides which repeat every 24, 12 and so on hours, and L_1, L_2 and so on for the equivalent lunar tides (the periods of these differ slightly from the solar tides because the Moon takes $24 \cdot 87$ hours to pass once around the Earth). The two periods of the Moon, $24 \cdot 87$ hours and $29 \cdot 53$ days, represent the time taken for the Earth to rotate until the Moon is vertically above some reference marker or observatory, and the time taken for the Moon to travel around the spinning Earth in its own orbit (from new Moon to new Moon). The first period differs slightly from twenty-four hours because by the time the Earth has rotated through 360 degrees, the Moon has moved on slightly in its own orbit. The S_2 tide dominates the pressure variations measured at the surface of the Earth, while the S_1 tide produces a more erratic effect on barometers reaching about half the size of the S_2 effect. All the other solar tides and all of the lunar tides were, until a few years ago, regarded by meteorologists as too small to play a part in affecting the weather of our planet.

There are a lot of unavoidable astronomical terms which creep into any discussion of the geometry of alignments of the Sun, Moon and planets; but they will be handy in the next chapter so this is a good time to get them sorted out. *Syzygy* is the time of either a new Moon or full Moon; it is particularly interesting because at both times the Sun, Moon and Earth are aligned, so that the Moon and Sun pull together on the Earth. The *synodic* period of the Moon, from full to new, is $29 \cdot 53$ days, while the exact orbital time of the Moon, from perigee to perigee (the closest approach to Earth) is the *anomalistic* period of $27 \cdot 55$ days. This is not really anomalistic; it just differs from the synodic period because between new Moons the Earth travels a little way around the Sun and the Moon's orbit always seems to be catching up. The *ecliptic* is the plane in which the average movements of the Sun, Moon and planets lie. It seems to be tilted at $23\frac{1}{2}$ degrees to the equator because the Earth leans over by that amount as it wobbles around the Sun.

Reports of correlations between the synodic period of the moon's orbit ($29 \cdot 53$ days) and precipitation on Earth are now beginning to receive attention. Glenn Brier, of the United States Weather Bureau, compiled an interesting study of the precipitation statistics during the 1960s. He had no problem in trying to relate the tidal effects of precipitation by a chain of cause and effect, because so little is known about what causes precipitation anyway that the exercise would have been pointless. We are again wandering in the realms of the empirical scientist, where important discoveries often take on their first misty shape before being captured and codified into physical laws. So Brier has studied just the geometry of the situation—how the positions of the Sun and the Moon, seen from the Earth, can be related to rainfall. If that sounds like astrology, it is; astrology is based upon the same empirical framework of observational astronomy as is modern astronomy. The difference is that we now understand at least the beginning of the way in which the positions of the planets can affect conditions far removed from them, for example by gravity, and we will accept only the empirical evidence which stands up to searching examination. Mere coincidence is not enough.

One of the first associations claimed between weather patterns and the Moon is a half-synodic period of $14 \cdot 765$ days in precipitation variations in the United States. Brier has looked at how this kind of variation occurs, and he found that the effect is greater at times of syzygy when the Moon is either full or new within two days of perigee and two days of crossing the ecliptic. This sounds complicated but all it really means is that the influence of the Moon on precipitation can be noticed only when Sun, Moon and Earth are aligned almost perfectly. As they move out of this in-line position, the anomalistic and nodical cycles (the nodical cycle of $27 \cdot 21$ days is the time the Moon takes between successive north-to-south crossings of the ecliptic) get further and further out of step with the synodic cycles and the $14 \cdot 765$ day variation is smeared out. When conditions were ideal—on sixty-one occasions from 1900 to 1962—precipitation over the United States was 20 per cent greater in the two days after syzygy than in the two days before.

Brier has also looked at daily variations. For the United States as a whole (excluding Hawaii), the most favorable times for precipitation on climatological grounds are 3 A.M. and 5 P.M. From sixty-three years of daily precipitation data it seems that maximum precipitation occurs on those days in the month when the moon passes the zenith just before these times there is more precipitation than other days in the month. All in all, Brier believes that tidal forces, in particular the L_2 tide, can trigger rainfall *when all other conditions are favorable*. The important factors are the distances to the Sun and the Moon, their alignment and their angles relative to the zenith (the point directly above an observer on Earth). All this tells us two things: small effects, ignored by meteorologists for years, can profoundly affect weather patterns on Earth; and planetary alignments, when conditions are favorable, can trigger surprisingly large affects since they can interact with a complex system which is already on the edge of stability. Now we are suitably armed to hunt the triggering influence on sunspot activity.

9 The Solar Sunspot Cycle and Alignment of the Planets

Several times now in our search for an earthquake trigger, we have encountered the influence of sunspots. Now we want to find what influence it is that activates sunspots to trigger earthquakes, and we should provide some details of what this influence might be. It seems that this is a good time to have a detailed look at exactly what sunspots are, and at the degrees of understanding astronomers have today about the peculiar eleven-year cycle of solar activity.

The Nature of Sunspots

Sunspots, as their name implies, are simply dark blotches or spots on the face of the Sun. These spots—there is usually at least one large spot and smaller flecks on the Sun at any time—can often be seen when the Sun is low down on the horizon and partly screened by a thin blanket of mist or fog. They were known to ancient Chinese, Japanese and Korean astronomers, and were reported by the Greek Theophratus in 300 B.C. But for 1900 years their existence was forgotten, and only in 1610 did Galileo rediscover sunspots when he invented the telescope. Galileo knew as well as we do that it would be extremely dangerous to look at the Sun directly through the focusing lenses of a telescope, and he devised the method of watching sunspots which is still the most widely used today. This method allows the image of the Sun's disk to be projected onto a white card behind the eyepiece of the telescope, and the astronomer watches this image of the Sun rather than the Sun itself.

The discovery made by Galileo caused consternation in the seventeenth century. At that time the Sun was regarded as a perfect body of pure fire, and it was almost heretical to suggest that this perfect body might be pitted with blemishes. Many people who observed the spots but were less bold argued that they might really be small, dark objects in orbit around the Sun. But with the development of the scientific school of thought this suggestion was soon dismissed for the half-hearted timid proposal that it was, and eventually the Sun, displaced from its position as a perfect fiery sphere burning at the center of the universe, was known in its true colors as an insignificant, spotty little star in the backwaters of a rather ordinary galaxy.

Even before astronomers had any inkling of what sunspots were, they used the spots to discover details of the Sun's behavior. Like the Earth, the Sun rotates on its axis, and the movement of sunspots from east to west (the same direction of rotation for all the planets orbiting the Sun) provides an indication of the speed of this rotation. Tracing the direction in which the spots move helps astronomers to locate the equator of the Sun, and it turns out that the Sun is tilted at an angle of about 7 degrees with respect to the plane of the Earth's orbit. Also, because the Sun is a gaseous body it spins faster at the equator, where its 'day' is twenty-five Earth days, than at the poles, where twenty-nine Earth days are required for the Sun to complete one revolution. The reason why sunspots are visible at all is that they are darker and cooler than the surrounding surface of the Sun. This darkness is deceptive, for even in a sunspot the amount of light radiated is 200,000 times more than we see reflected by the full Moon.

This lower temperature of sunspots allows the negative electrons and positive ions which form the plasma, or hot gas, in the Sun to combine briefly into neutral atoms inside the spots. All atoms radiate light at certain discrete frequencies, or spectral lines, and variations in these spectral lines reveal a great deal to astronomers on Earth about the conditions inside the spot. One of the most important discoveries is that the line spectrum from a sunspot contains features exactly equivalent to those seen in laboratory experiments when atoms are held in strong magnetic fields. Obviously, sunspots too are regions of strong magnetism—but immensely stronger than the Earth's magnetic fields. The magnetic field in a sunspot reaches thousands of gauss but the Earth's magnetic field is less than one gauss.

Spectroscopic astronomy is even able to reveal whether a particular sunspot is associated with a south magnetic pole or a north magnetic pole. This magnetism follows a regular pattern, and almost invariably sunspots are found in nearby pairs, one of each magnetic polarity almost like the poles of a bar magnet. In a given solar cycle the north magnetic pole will always orient to one side in the northern hemisphere of the Sun and to the other side of the solar southern hemisphere. When there are many spots in a group, the number of north and south magnetic poles cancel out in pairs. On occasions when one spot is seen by itself there is always a region of opposite magnetic polarity—an invisible spot—detectable nearby.

Sunspots do not last for long, even in terms of the

period of rotation of the Sun. Their patterns on the solar surface can change noticeably within a few hours; and only the largest sunspots with the strongest magnetic fields survive to be tracked during a complete revolution of the Sun. But although individual spots are short-lived, successive spots are formed according to a very clear-cut behavior pattern, and it is this regularly changing pattern of behavior which is known as the solar cycle. It is not simply that there are more spots on the Sun's surface every eleven years or so; the exact positions of the spots relative to the equator and to one another also change in a regular way.

The Solar Cycle of Sunspot Activity

After a few hundred years of regular observations of sunspots, from the time of Galileo up to the nineteenth century, astronomers noticed a regular pattern. This cycle takes an average of eleven years, but can take as little as nine years or as much as sixteen years. At the beginning of any cycle a few sunspots form well away from the equator, at latitudes of around 30 degrees. In both northern and southern hemispheres the spot leading any pair (that is, to the west) is slightly nearer the equator. On average, the leaders of spot pairs in each northern solar hemisphere all have the same polarity, but the northern leaders are of opposite magnetic polarity to the southern leaders. Towards the peak of activity of a solar cycle more spots are formed, and these tend to be born closer and closer to the equator. By the end of the cycle many spots are being formed very close to the equator on either solar hemisphere. Then the activity stops and soon the eleven-year pattern of behaviour begins to repeat, with a few spots being formed at latitudes of 30 degrees or so. But that is not quite the end of the story, because in the next cycle the polarity of the leaders in each hemisphere is the opposite of what it was in the previous cycle. Perhaps it is more accurate to say that the eleven-year solar cycles are really paired in twenty-two-year cycles.

This is fine as far as it goes. Obviously there must be some very important, fundamental process underlying all this sunspot activity, whose regular changes have been monitored for more than 350 years. But what is it? Astronomers simply do not know. Indeed, they do not know in detail just how the strong magnetic fields in sunspots are produced, although it seems fairly certain that they must be related to strong electric currents—ten million million amperes or more—flowing via the charged particles in the Sun's atmosphere. In the study of sunspots, anyway, we are still very much back in the realms of empirical science, where we might be able to predict what will happen next year by studying the patterns of behavior of the past three centuries but where we can make no prediction based on an understanding of the physical laws which sunspots obey.

Variations in the Solar Cycle and Their Causes

Just as the length of the solar cycle varies about the average length of roughly eleven years, maximum amplitude of spottiness of the Sun varies in a seemingly irregular way. The spots have been likened to solar weather—a visible manifestation of powerful underlying forces—as terrestrial weather is the visible effect of global movements of air in response to the rotation of the Earth, the heating of the Sun, and other effects.

We have seen in chapter 8 how periodic changes caused by tidal forces of the Sun and Moon affect weather on the Earth; so it would be no real surprise to find that the positions of the planets are associated with the changes in the intensity of the Sun's sunspot 'weather'. But there are so many planetary orbital periodicities to unravel, and the changes in the amplitude of solar cycle maximum are so complex, that it has taken the best part of a century for any kind of understanding to emerge of the complex interaction of the whole Solar System.

Modern Observations and Theories

Over the past four decades several things have combined to make for an improved empirical understanding of the relations between planetary alignments and sunspots. Forty years of new data is a considerable amount even considering the time it takes for the outer planets to travel once around the Sun—the 'year' of Jupiter is $11 \cdot 86$ terrestrial years, that of Saturn $29 \cdot 5$ years, Uranus orbits the Sun every $84 \cdot 02$ years, Neptune once in $164 \cdot 8$ years, and tiny Pluto, the outermost planet, once in 248 years. Electronic computers have made it much less tedious to work out the exact alignments of the planets at any time, working either forwards or backwards from their present positions. Although sunspots have been studied by many people more or less continuously since Galileo rediscovered them in 1610, it is only since the latter part of the nineteenth century that records of sunspot numbers have been available for every day of the year. Finally, astronomer-historians have now unearthed many early records of sunspot activity which can be compared with the computed planetary positions appropriate for the time when the records were made. In the late 1960s and early 1970s these many lines of attack began to yield important empirical evidence indicating how important the alignments of all the planets of the Solar System, and not just the Earth and Venus, are for the occurrence of sunspots.

One line of approach emphasizes the theory that the variation in the distances of the planets from the Sun must moderate the size of the effect they can have on sunspots. After all, if this is a tidal gravitational influence it will depend on the inverse of the cube of the distance from the Sun to each planet, as well as directly on the actual mass of the planet. We encountered these ideas earlier in chapter 6, while discussing the tidal influence of the Sun and the Moon upon the Earth. However, we will now examine the details of this tidal influence on the Sun by Mercury and other planets. Mercury is one of the smallest planets, with a diameter of only some 4000 km and mass less than one-tenth of that of the Earth. If it were at the same distance from the Sun as is the Earth, we might expect its gravitational influence to be ten times less; however, because Mercury is much less than half of the distance of the Earth from the Sun its gravitational influence is many times more effective. Multiplying the two effects (size and distance) indicates that Mercury's gravitational influence on the Sun is about the same as the Earth's influence. In fact the effect can be greater still because Mercury has quite an elliptical orbit. At closest approach to the Sun (perihelion) it is within 45·5 million km, compared with the Earth's average distance from the Sun of 149·6 million km (this Earth–Sun average distance is called the Astronomical Unit of distance, or AU). At aphelion, the furthest point of Mercury's orbit from the Sun is 70 million km.

The time taken for Mercury to travel once around the Sun is only eighty-eight days. Nevertheless, Mercury is the *slowest* moving planet relative to a point on the Sun's rotating surface, and its contribution provides a small, high frequency effect superimposed on the action of the other planets. So in the short time of moving from aphelion to perihelion in forty-four days, one would expect a considerable change in the amount of Mercury's influence on sunspots—if there is any such influence at all! The change in the tidal influence of Mercury on the Sun is 3 to 1 in that short time; but sunspots take up to six weeks to form and move around the Sun (or rather, the Sun revolves every twenty-five days, carrying the spots embedded in its surface). Picking out any influence of Mercury on sunspots involves very careful mathematical analysis of the statistics, using a high-speed electronic computer to study observations made over many years.

Influence of the Planet Mercury on Sunspots

One such study of Mercury's influence on the Sun was carried out in 1967 by Dr. E. K. Bigg of Sydney, Australia. Dr. Bigg realized that picking out a 'Mercury effect' from the many complexities of the variations of sunspot activity is similar to a problem commonly encountered by radio engineers, of having to detect a radio signal at a particular frequency from a background of other signals and radio noise. If the exact frequency of the radio signal which is being searched for is known, then it is possible to pick the signal out even when it is very weak and hidden in a great deal of background noise. The method radio engineers use in such a situation is first to narrow down their search to a band of frequencies around the expected frequency, then to filter out noise while narrowing the band of frequencies. The final test (called a correlation technique) asks if the characteristics of the signal being received—notably its variation with time—are just those expected for the kind of signal which is known to be being transmitted. Dr. Bigg has used the same step-by-step approach in studying the relation between Mercury's orbit and the Sun and solar activity.

By taking daily sunspot numbers between 1850 and 1960, Dr. Bigg made a 'spectrum' containing information about many variations at many frequencies. The test frequency corresponds to the exact orbital period of Mercury around the Sun (87·969 days) so the 'spectrum' was first divided into equal lengths of exactly this period. Dr. Bigg divided each 87·969-day portion of the 'spectrum' into 100 equal parts and used a computer to compare the number of sunspots which occurred during each first subdivision, each second subdivision and so on. If the 'spectrum' contains a periodic variation of 87·969 days, there should be a correlation between each corresponding subdivision. This is just what the computer study reveals. After testing for more than one hundred different frequencies in the 'spectrum', Dr. Bigg found that the only one which could have any physical significance in 460 orbits of Mercury about the Sun was also the one which showed the best correlation in this test. The accuracy of this test was so good that the correlation would not have been found if the solar cycle variations occurred with a period different from that of Mercury by only as little as one part in 5000, or one-tenth of a cycle in the 460 studied. The agreement is indeed impressive.

But Dr. Bigg did not stop there. He went on to compare the sunspot numbers recorded from 1850 to 1960 with the positions of the Earth, Venus and Jupiter in their orbits in relation to the position of Mercury. It would have been asking too much of the computing technique he used to compare all the planetary positions together, but he found that each planet modifies the Mercury effect on the Sun in much the same way that the position of the Earth in its orbit modifies the comparable Venus effect.

When another planet (Venus, Earth or Jupiter) is on the same side of the Sun as Mercury during Mercury's closest approach to the Sun (perihelion) the Mercury effect is twice as large as when the planet is on the opposite side of the Sun.

This can only mean that a real physical effect is present and that the same effect is acting for all the planets. What could this be other than a tidal influence resulting from the gravitational attraction of the planets on the Sun? Probably what happens is that when a sunspot region is building up towards a period of activity, the transition from 'no spot' to 'spot' can be pushed over some critical value, or held back, by the periodically changing tidal influence of Mercury, even though that tidal influence may be much smaller than the total forces involved in creating sunspots. It is most unlikely that Mercury directly causes the creation of sunspots, but its influence probably acts like a final straw or trigger.

Dr. Bigg's 1967 study provided a landmark in the development of an understanding of sunspots. There is no longer any room for doubt that at least one planet influences the activity of the Sun; we also have a hint of the significance of other planetary alignments to a complex world of solar activity. What happens when the Solar System is considered as a whole? How drastically can the sunspot cycle be affected when three, four or more planets all align themselves on the same side of the Sun? These questions assume a pressing significance now that we have found the key which might unlock the secret of the variation of the cycle of solar activity. For planetary alignment is also the key to the trigger for unusually high levels of terrestrial earthquake activity. It turns out that there will be a very rare alignment of the planets, with all of them pulling together on the Sun, in the early 1980s. Will this produce an even more dramatic effect in terms of sunspot activity and earthquakes? The answer comes from another analysis of historical records of sunspot activity.

The Total Influence of Planetary Alignments on the Sun's Activity

We are now dealing with work which has only been carried out very recently. The development of our understanding of how the planets influence the Sun parallels in a remarkable way the development of our understanding of the forces which shape the continents. This story would be incomprehensible without both pieces of the theory we have developed; both parts, being developed independently, reached their climax early in the 1970s, ready to be fitted together into a whole which is very much more than the sum of its parts.

Very late in 1972 Professor K. D. Wood, of the University of Colorado, reported, in the scientific journal *Nature,* his detailed study of how most of the planets in the Solar System influence the Sun, and in particular how they influence the intensity of sunspots during successive eleven-year sunspot cycles. Professor Wood did not include Mercury in his study, because he was seeking long-term influences which affect several solar cycles of eleven years. A three-month variation due to Mercury would affect the activity only within each cycle, not the average sunspot activity throughout eleven or more years. Apart from Mercury, the main tidal influence on the Sun comes from Venus and the Earth because they move in close orbits to the Sun, and from Jupiter which is so large that its influence is pronounced even though it is much further from the Sun. The average influence of each planet can be normalized into units of the tide raised by the Earth on the Sun. If the magnitude of that tide is 1 unit, then Venus tides average a height of 2·13 units and Jupiter's tides average 2·28 units. (Mercury, neglected but not forgotten, averages 0·5 and 1·8 at the two extremes of its very elliptical orbit.)

Professor Wood has elaborated on the various tidal influences due to Venus, Earth and Jupiter in detail. When the Earth and Venus are in conjunction (on the same side of the Sun) or in opposition (on opposite sides of the Sun) they combine to raise a total tide on the Sun some 50 per cent greater than the largest tide ever raised by Jupiter. When all three planets are aligned their combined tidal effects add together on the Sun's surface. It is easy to show that the Earth and Venus are in conjunction every 1·8 years, and in opposition 0·8 years after each conjunction, while in 0·8 years the Earth moves about 264° in its orbit relative to Jupiter. These straightforward pieces of observational information enable Professor Wood to calculate the height of the gravitational tide raised on the Sun by the three planets at any time in the future or past, starting from the known positions of the planets in 1972. This he has done, measuring tidal force again in units of the average tide raised on the Sun by the Earth. It was then a simple matter for him to compare the tidal height with sunspot activity over the nineteenth and twentieth centuries, when detailed records have been kept. The results are illustrated graphically in figure 18 and include Professor Wood's forecast for the time between 1972 to the end of this century. The relation between sunspot activity and these tidal influences is completely beyond question. The predictions of tidal height are exact, of course, and only the data on sunspot numbers remain approximate, since reliable sunspot numbers are only available back to 1800. But indications of the years of sunspot maximum and sunspot minimum ('peak' and 'valley' dates) can be obtained from historical records right back to the time of Galileo, two centuries earlier still.

Dr. E. Opik has shown that Wood's tidal gravitational effects should raise a tidal flow on the Sun with a velocity of 93 cm/sec (compared to 300 cm/sec for lunar tides on the Earth)—not at all negligible! At this velocity and with the solar gravity acceleration 27·6 times the terrestrial, Opik calculates a tidal displacement over one-half of the sun's rotation of 560 km in a horizontal direction which may suffice to trigger off some unspecified instabilities leading to sunspot activity. No one has yet proposed a specific and detailed mechanism for the interaction of planetary resonances and solar activity characteristics. This would require a complete magnetic-hydrodynamical treatment of the external tidal and the inertial forces within the Sun. The matter is complicated by factors like tides on the Sun, raised by planets at right angles to each other, tend to cancel each other near the solar equator, though they still reinforce each other at solar latitudes greater than 55° (neglecting the 7° inclination of the planetary plane to the solar axis). Dr. Opik calculated the probability of chance coincidence of the sunspot maximum keeping to within one-half year of the Peak of Wood's tidal cycle (shown on p. 127) as one chance in 1230, enough to consider the correlation of these two periodic phenomena as real.

These records provide further impressive evidence linking planetary alignment and sunspots. The corresponding 'peak' dates are compared with dates of tidal maxima for the first twenty solar cycles since 1600 in table 1. When these data are combined with the corresponding plots in figure 18, we cover over three and a half centuries of observation. Between 1600–1972, the dates of tidal height and sunspot maximum rarely differ from each other by more than a few months. This difference could be due to some other physical effect, for remember Professor Wood has calculated only the influence of the alignment of the three most significant planets, while neglecting the other planets and the internal processes going on within the Sun itself.

The most exciting prediction of this investigation is still to come. In the same way that Dr. Bigg compared

Table 1. Comparison of sunspot cycle peak dates with dates of peak tidal fluctuation.

Sunspot cycle No.	Sunspot peak date	Tidal peak date
—13	1604·5	1605·4
—12	1615·5	1617·5
—11	1626·0	1628·3
—10	1639·7	1639·5
—9	1649·0	1650·5
—8	1660·0	1661·5

Sunspot cycle No.	Sunspot peak date	Tidal peak date
—7	1675·0	1672·1
—6	1685·0	1683·3
—5	1693·0	1693·7
—4	1705·5	1705·1
—3	1718·2	1716·2
—2	1727·5	1727·0
—1	1738·7	1738·4
0	1750·1	1749·8
1	1761·5	1760·6
2	1769·8	1772·2
3	1778·5	1782·8
4	1788·2	1794·1
5	1804·8	1805·6
6	1816·4	1816·6
7	1830·0	1827·0
8	1837·2	1838·2
9	1848·3	1848·7
10	1860·2	1859·5
11	1870·7	1871·0
12	1884·0	1881·0
13	1893·9	1893·1
14	1906·3	1904·5
15	1917·7	1915·9
16	1928·4	1927·1
17	1937·6	1937·9
18	1947·5	1949·5
19	1958·2	1960·7
20	1969·3	1971·3
	Forecast	
21	1982·0	1982·0
22	1993·4	1992·9
23	2002·1	2004·1
24	2014·0	2014·5
25	2025·6	2026·1
26	2036·1	2037·6
27	2048·3	2048·3
28	2056·6	2059·1
29	2071·4	2070·9
30	2079·5	2081·5

Sunspot cycle No.	Sunspot peak date	Tidal peak date
31	2093·6	2092·6
32	2104·4	2103·9

Average cycle lengths are: sunspots 11·05 yr, planet tides 11·08 yr.

1750 is chosen as 'year zero' arbitrarily.
These data are taken from Wood, K. D., *Nature*, 240, 91; 1972. They extend the information in figure 18 back to the period when only the years of sunspot maximum were recorded, not the actual number of spots seen each year. By extrapolating the data, and calculating future tides raised on the Sun, Professor Wood has produced a prediction of solar activity for cycles beyond number 20.

---

corresponding subdivisions of Mercury's period to find a correlation, the 370 years of sunspot observations can be divided into interesting periods and subdivisions to see whether or not the period chosen has any physical significance. When this is done it seems that the sunspot numbers follow a repeated pattern roughly every 170 to 180 years; that is, the solar cycle from 1923 to 1934 can be superimposed upon the cycle from 1755 to 1766. Annoyingly, there is just not quite enough information available to study this aspect of the problem reliably; since 1800 we have had just one such long cycle. But look at table 1 again and recall the great solar flare of 1959. The exact peak of the corresponding cycle was in 1958 and there were 201 sunspots that year—more than in any other year of the table. In 1788, at the height of the corresponding solar cycle 170 years before, the sunspot number was 141—again one of the highest numbers of sunspots recorded. The preceding peaks, in 1947 and 1778, were 152 and 151 respectively, both higher than average, and three cycles before, in 1928 and 1750, the peaks were more normal with 78 and 92 sunspots. It is possible to sit for hours picking out such relations; but we can go one better than Professor Wood and pinpoint a periodic planetary alignment which occurs with just the right frequency to explain this effect.

Sunspots and the Solar System Center of Mass

In its simple form, the tidal theory may not be correct, although Wood's work in particular is certainly intriguing. But there are other possible mechanisms which might explain the influence of planetary alignments on solar activity. Jose and Sleeper found a 180-year period due to resonances of the four giant planets (Jupiter, Saturn, Uranus and Neptune), and suggest that the 11-year cycle is due to resonances in the periods of the inner planets. Sleeper finds both 80- and 30-year sunspot periods associated with climatic changes on Earth; Cohen and Lintz find the now familiar 180-year period in sunspot records, and suggest that this is a 'beat' effect of the 11-year period and a 9.8-year period, interacting like two nearby musical notes struck together. Where could such a 9.8-year period come from? According to Sleeper, this is just half the synodic period of resonance caused by Jupiter-Saturn conjunction—we are back again to the giant planets, and especially Jupiter!

The wealth and variety of evidence is remarkable, although all too often it has either been ignored or kept quiet by the discoverers themselves, afraid perhaps, of ridicule. After the first edition of this book appeared, it turned out that the NASA colleagues of one of us, working in the same building, had carried out an unpublished study showing an increase of up to 20 per cent in solar activity at times of these infrequent conjunctions of the Solar System's two largest planets, leading to the perhaps not entirely facetious suggestion that the book should be retitled "The Jupiter-Saturn Effect." In the light of these new (to us) developments, one alternative model in particular seems a strong rival to the direct tidal theory. That is the possibility that changes in the position of the Solar System center of mass play a significant part in determining the level of solar activity.

As recently as 1975, R. M. Wood (the son of Professor K. D. Wood) has suggested that tides are likely to be less important than effects on the oblate spinning Sun, while Dauvillier suggests that movements of the Sun around the center of mass provide the key influence on that system. If we consider the movement of the Sun relative to the center of mass of the Solar System, we find that it follows a looping orbit over a distance comparable to the solar diameter and that the patterns in the looping movement recur with periods of 11, 30, 80 and 180 years, due to the varying pull from the planets. As the planets, especially the giants, move around the Sun they swing it backwards and forwards and around like circling ice skaters holding hands with one another. It is quite permissible to use a reference system in which we choose to view the motion from the center of the Sun, when we would "see" the center of mass looping around the Sun, sometimes below its surface and sometimes outside the Sun entirely; this is the usual way of looking at things, since we are used to thinking of the Sun as our fixed reference, but it does not give the best physical picture. The center of mass is the true center of the Solar System, and the looping orbit of the Sun around that center has real physical significance, producing the same kind of 'centrifugal' and 'coriolis' forces that a human being would feel when trying to walk across the center of a spinning merry-go-round. Events on the surface of the Sun are strongly influenced by convection in its interior, and the convection is known to be sensitive to changes in the gravity gradient and effects such as coriolis and centrifugal forces. Dauvillier has calculated that there is a clear proportionality of the activity of the solar cycle (expressed by Wolf sunspot numbers) and the distance between the center of the Sun and the center of the Solar System on which the centrifugal force depends. He predicts that the next solar maximum, which is our great concern here, will be only slightly less than the biggest in this century, which occurred in 1959.

Torque effects have also been discussed, notably by R. M. Wood and by Blizard, in connection with the link between planets and sunspots, with partial success when applied to the 22 year cycle. Perhaps more than one of these mechanisms is operating, but there seems to us no doubt that some physical mechanism does indeed link the positions of the planets to solar activity—and it is perhaps particularly significant that essentially all of these suggested will be producing a strong influence on the key dates between 1982 and 1984 when the greatest number of conjunctions occur.

The Planetary Alignments from 1982 to 1984

Between 1977 and 1984 the planets of the Solar System will be moving into an unusual alignment in which every planet is in conjunction with every other planet; that is, all the planets will be aligned on the same side of the Sun. Such an alignment occurs only once every 179 years, less than the period of Pluto's orbit (248 years). This occurs because the eight planets move faster than Pluto and so get round the Sun ready for another alignment more quickly than Pluto does. Nep-

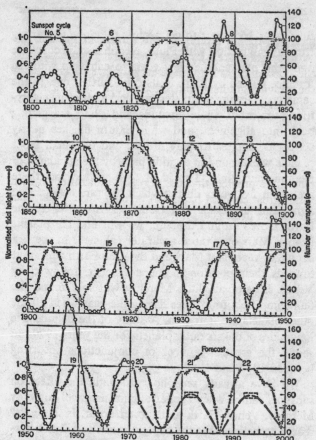

FIGURE 18. Variation of the calculated tidal height at the sub-Jupiter point due to the Earth and Venus at conjunction (or opposition) (dashed line) compared with the observed number of sunspots (solid line) since 1880. (From Wood, K. D., *Nature*, 240, 91; 1973. Courtesy of *Nature*.) Wood's predictions for future sunspot activity can be taken as accurate indicators of the dates of sunspot maxima to the end of this century. However, he takes no account of the rare planetary alignment due in 1982: we believe that the sunspot peak in that cycle will be much greater than he suggests. This is the key to the trigger effect on the San Andreas fault.

tune takes 165 years to get around the Sun; so starting
from a conjunction with Pluto, Neptune must complete
one orbit plus another few years to catch up with the
distance moved by Pluto in its orbit further out. In the
same way Uranus completes two and a bit of its eighty-
four year orbits while Neptune and Pluto are getting
back into alignment, and while Saturn finishes nearly
six orbits, Jupiter roughly fifteen, and the small inner
planets whirl round at a giddy pace by the standards of
Neptune and Pluto. This is why we can say that there
are about five years during which the rare conjunction
is building up. Each year from 1977 to 1982, as the
Earth moves around the Sun, we will find the planets
beyond Mars ever more accurately aligned. In the last
couple of years first Mars and then the Earth will move
towards their position in the alignment, followed by
Venus. Last of all, little Mercury will spin round the
Sun completely four times during the year when all the
other planets are lining up. A study of the heliocentric
longitudes of the six outer planets for the years 1977–86
shows the greatest number of conjunctions occurring
between 1982 and 1984.

We have already seen how dramatic the effect on
sunspots can be when similar alignments involving only
Mercury, Venus, Earth and Jupiter occur. Is there any
reason to believe that the superalignments will not produce even more dramatic effects? Certainly, dramatic
effects have been expected from such auspicious events
as long as man has studied the stars. Some astrologers
mark the beginning of a new age by the occasion of the
grand alignment—when Jupiter aligns with Mars and
the Moon is in the Seventh House, the Age of Aquarius
begins. The Age of Aquarius will be, we are told, a
time of peace and love. But will it be ushered in by a
major slip of the San Andreas Fault and a wave of

earthquake activity around the globe, unprecedented since seismology became a true science?

It is not only astrologers who are fascinated by the alignment of the planets. Such a grand alignment provides a rare opportunity for space vehicles to be sent on a 'grand tour' of two, three or more of the outer planets. Current NASA plans are for two Mariner class Saturn orbiters to be launched in 1985, followed the next year by two Mariner spacecraft which will use gravity assist to fly past Uranus and on to Neptune. It would be the literal truth to say that the launch dates of these space probes, which depend critically on the exact positions of the planets, are determined by NASA's expert team of latter-day astrologers!

So the next time of sunspot maximum will occur early in 1982, as Professor Wood has predicted (a view shared also by Drs. T. J. Cohen and P. R. Lintz in a study published in *Nature* of August 1974). If the tidal influence of the planets neglected in Professor Wood's study is calculated, it turns out to be rather small. We might suppose, then, that the grand alignment of 1982 would be no more dramatic than other alignments involving Venus, Earth and Jupiter, although these are impressive enough. But a remarkable study published twenty years ago, in 1954, hints that this may not be the case.

After World War II the study of radio communications entered a new era. It was known that the activity of the Sun disturbed radio communications—we now know that this occurs through the sort of interaction of solar particles with the Earth's magnetosphere discussed in chapters 7 and 8. Many radio engineers became interested in predicting 'radio weather'; in other words, they wanted to predict solar activity so that they would know in advance when radio communications were likely to be difficult. Working in isolation from astronomers, the radio engineers tackled the problem in a completely empirical fashion. All they wanted was an effective way to predict the influence of the Sun on radio signals on the Earth; if their ideas conflict with any established beliefs about the Sun, just too bad. Well, they found such a 'radio weather' predictor and it did run counter to some cherished astronomical beliefs, which may be why the results of these studies are not too widely known among astronomers. However, the prediction scheme was trusted by RCA Communications Inc., who financed the study of radio weather forecasting not through any scientific altruism but because of hardheaded business sense. Dr. John Nelson reported the results of his study in 1954, and in spite of their remarkable predictions they seem to have laid dormant ever since, at least as far as astronomers are concerned.

Dr. Nelson and his team soon found evidence of the influence of planets on sunspots—the sort of evidence we have already discussed for Venus, Earth, Mercury and Jupiter. But moving rapidly on from this look at the Solar System as a whole, they investigated relationships between planetary alignments and radio weather during the quiet period of the Sun from 1951 to 1953, when there were very few sunspots. They found that alignments of 0 degrees (planets on the same side of the Sun), 90 degrees and 270 degrees (when planets and the Sun form a right-angled triangle) and 180 degrees (planets in line with the Sun but on opposite sides) are significant indicators of the radio weather. When *any three* of the Sun's nine planets are aligned like this, there are radio disturbances even when there are few sunspots (that is, during the years between sunspot peaks). More severe radio disturbances were related to alignments of five or six of the nine planets at these angles at the same time, to within a few days. The most impressive radio disturbances occurred when one of the inner planets (Mercury, Venus, Earth or Mars) was linked in such a geometric arrangement with the Sun and one or more slower moving planets (Jupiter, Saturn, Uranus, Neptune or Pluto).

Sunspots, of course, are just the most visible part of solar activity. Cosmic rays from the Sun are constantly streaming past the Earth, and variations in cosmic rays will affect the ionosphere, and radio propagation, even when the effects are far too small to change the atmospheric circulation, let along change the Earth's spin and produce earthquakes. Although Pluto itself is probably of very little importance in the chain from planets to solar activity to earthquakes, Nelson's remarkable work shows just how the whole Solar System interacts to affect facets of our daily lives.

We are concerned only with the most dramatic disturbances of the Sun's equilibrium, the sunspots, since to trigger earthquakes we need great disturbances of the ionosphere and the Earth's atmospheric circulation (far more than is needed to disrupt the propagation of radio waves). Perhaps there are other factors also at work, as suggested by the radio weather studies of Dr. Nelson and his team of engineers at RCA. But of one thing we can be absolutely sure; the unusual planetary alignment is inexorably approaching and it will affect the activity of the Sun. We have come a long way in our search for a trigger, from California to Jupiter, but it looks as though we have found it.

We suspect from the work of Sleeper and others that the sunspot cycle now in progress is a long one of 13 years; and if Dauvillier is correct, it will peak with strong activity and sunspot numbers reaching around

160. From time to time between 1982 and 1984 we imagine that there will be bursts of very strong activity associated with the unusual series of alignments; streams of charged particles flowing out past the planets, including the Earth, will be affected by these bursts of activity may well produce a pronounced effect on the overall circulation of the weather patterns (especially at high latitudes), as discussed in Appendix B—and this activity will occur whichever of the physical processes or combination of process which dominates is responsible.

Finally, the last link in the chain, movements of large masses of the atmosphere will agitate regions of geologic instability into life. There will be many earthquakes, large and small, around susceptible regions of the globe. And one region where one of the greatest fault systems lies today under a great strain, long overdue for a giant leap forward and just awaiting the necessary kick, is California. The situation is not directly comparable with that of 1803, the last time such a planetary alignment occurred, because we have no way of knowing how much strain the San Andreas fault was then under. Most likely, it will be the Los Angeles section of the fault to move this time. Possibly, it will be the San Francisco area which has a major quake. The prospect of both these sections of the fault moving at once hardly bears thinking about. In any case, a major earthquake will herald one of the greatest disasters of modern times.

10 Preparation for the Next
    Great Californian Earthquake

Any thinking person who lives near the San Francisco and Los Angeles regions of the San Andreas fault must be concerned by the prospect of another major earthquake in the near future. Until very recently it might have been possible to argue—but without very much conviction—that it probably will not happen until we are all dead, so why worry. But we have now seen how inexorably the evidence points to disaster not more than a few years away. What exactly is likely to happen? And how can those who must live in the danger zones prepare for the worst?

It is some comfort to find that government departments and official agencies are aware of the dangers, and are making plans for the most effective possible action when the earthquake comes. In the case of a really serious earthquake, however, the plans of man seem almost pitifully inadequate. Ironically, too, most attention in this respect has focused on San Francisco, where the memory of the 18 April 1906 shock remains. In fact, our search extending over the whole of our Solar System indicates that the Los Angeles region is more likely to suffer the next major jerk in the San Andreas fault, because there the fault has been dormant since 1856.

Official Preparations for San Francisco Bay Earthquakes

The first concern of the authorities in preparing for major earthquakes in California is, of course, to save lives and assist survivors. In a paper presented to the American Association for the Advancement of Science in 1974, Drs. T. Atwater and P. Molnar of MIT pointed out that the section of the San Andreas fault near San Francisco and to the North does not appear to have slipped substantially since 1906. During the 1906 earthquake the fault moved an average of 4 meters. If the San Andreas is absorbing most of the 5cm/year they expect the potential for an earthquake of the same size as in 1906 will have developed after 80 years, i.e. around 1986—a striking independent verdict in view of the predictions made in this book. One of the most detailed plans for such contingency operations was prepared in 1972 by the National Oceanic and Atmospheric Administration Environmental Research Laboratories, for the Office of Emergency Preparedness. Its stated purpose is to provide that Office and the State of California with 'a rational basis for planning earthquake disaster relief and recovery operations in the San Francisco Bay area'. In order to achieve this objective, the report predicts the effects of earthquakes of different magnitudes centered on different parts of the San Andreas and Hayward faults—in fact the Hayward fault, which parallels the San Andreas for a short distance just inland from the Bay, is a region of continuing creep and a most unlikely site for really catastrophic jumps, which are caused by the stick-slip motion we looked at in chapter 4. But before any predictions could be made, the NOAA team who compiled the report first had to analyze the effects of earthquakes which have occurred in the Bay area in historic times. A quite remarkable discovery emerges from this analysis.

The report itself is not concerned with predicting when or even where great earthquakes will occur. Its role is to create an awareness of what needs to be done, and what it will be possible to do, when the next such quake comes. Even if the NOAA had been concerned with earthquake prediction, they would not have known about the sunspot effect at the time their report was prepared. So their choice of earthquakes as models on which to base their calculations of the effects of such disasters is completely independent of the ideas we have developed in this book. Seventeen 'major historical earthquakes' are referred to in the report, all of which occurred since 1836, and all within about 240 km of the Golden Gate Bridge. Of these, eight were centered within a radius of 80 km from the entrance of the Bay. *Every one of these eight earthquakes occurred within two years of one or another of the dates of sunspot maximum given in Table I.* This includes the great 1906 earthquake. The dates of these events are 1836, 1838, 1861, 1868, 1892 (twice) and 1906.

Between 80 and 160 km from the Golden Gate, southeast along the fault in the region of active creep which we described in detail in chapter 3, there have been several historic earthquakes which are deemed important enough to be mentioned in the NOAA report. All of these were about as large as the smallest of the eight large historic quakes closer to the Bay, and just two of them occurred within two years of a time of sunspot maximum. The last two earthquakes mentioned in this study were each about 240 km from the Bay entrance, one to the southeast which occurred in 1885 (there was a sunspot maximum in 1884), and one to the northwest, off the coast, which occurred in 1898, halfway between two sunspot peak dates.

If we ignore the two furthest events from the Bay, we are left with a very striking result: in the immediate Bay area, eight quakes all near sunspot peak dates; in the next area out from the Bay, seven quakes in the same period of history, but only two near sunspot peak dates. We already know that the character of the San Andreas fault changes from continuous creep to jerky slip-stick movement in the Bay area (see chapter 3 and figure 8, page 31), and we have predicted that the jerks might be triggered by sunspot activity. The quite unbiased statistics from the official Office of Emergency Preparedness report lend eloquent testimony to the truth of these ideas.

With this additional support for the sunspot–earthquake link hinting again at the ominous significance of 1982, what would be the effect on human life if the quake struck the San Francisco Bay area, our second greatest area of risk after Los Angeles?

Earthquakes are the most difficult of all natural disasters to counter, both because of their indiscriminate effects and because they provide no warning, unlike, say, hurricanes or large-scale floods. Whereas even in a major fire in the heart of a city there remain areas nearby in which the injured can be tended and from which the disaster can be fought, in a great earthquake there may be few suitable buildings remaining to act as hospitals, and fire-fighters and other disaster workers will be hampered by broken water mains, impassable streets and so on.

As with the Beaufort scale of wind speeds, there is an easily understood scale by which earthquake strength can be measured. This is the Modified Mercalli scale, reproduced in table 2, on which the San Francisco earthquake of 1906 reached an intensity of XI; the energy released in it was the equivalent of more than the total food energy used by the entire present population of the Earth in one year. This scale quantifies the damage caused by an earthquake and so is particu-

Table 2. Modified Mercalli Intensity Scale

I. Not felt. Marginal and long-period effects of large earthquakes.

II. Felt by persons at rest, on upper floors, or favorably placed.

III. Felt indoors. Hanging objects swing. Vibration like passing of light trucks. Duration estimated. May not be recognized as an earthquake.

IV. Hanging objects swing. Vibration like passing of heavy trucks; or sensation of a jolt like a heavy ball striking the walls. Stationary automobiles rock. Windows, dishes, doors rattle. Glasses clink. Crockery clashes. In the upper range of IV wooden walls and frames creak.

V. Felt outdoors; direction estimated. Sleepers wakened. Liquids disturbed, some spilled. Small unstable objects displaced or upset. Doors swing, close, open. Shutters, pictures move. Pendulum clocks stop, start change rate.

VI. Felt by all. Many frightened and run outdoors. Persons walk unsteadily. Windows, dishes, glassware broken. Knick-knack, books, etc., fall off shelves. Pictures fall off walls. Furniture moved or overturned. Weak plaster cracked. Small bells ring (church, school). Trees, bushes shaken (visibly, or heard to rustle).

VII. Difficult to stand. Noticed by drivers of automobiles. Hanging objects quiver. Furniture broken. Weak chimneys broken at roof line. Fall of plaster, loose bricks, stones, tiles, cornices (also unbraced parapets and architectural ornaments). Waves on ponds; water turbid with mud. Small slides and caving in along sand or gravel banks. Large bells ring. Concrete irrigation ditches damaged.

VIII. Steering of automobiles affected. Fall of stucco and some masonry walls. Twisting, fall of chimneys, factory stacks, monuments, towers, elevated tanks. Frame houses moved on foundations if not bolted down; loose panel walls thrown out.

Decayed piling broken off. Branches broken off from trees. Changes in flow or temperature of springs and wells. Cracks in wet ground and on steep slopes.

IX.   General panic. General damage to foundations. Frame structures, if not bolted, shifted off foundations. Frames racked. Serious damage to reservoirs. Underground pipes broken. Conspicuous cracks in ground. In alluviated areas sand and mud ejected, earthquake fountains, sand craters.

X.   Most masonry and frame structures destroyed with their foundations. Some well-built wooden structures and bridges destroyed. Serious damage to dams, dikes, embankments. Large landslides. Water thrown on banks of canals, rivers, lakes, etc. Sand and mud shifted horizontally on beaches and flat land. Rails bent slightly.

XI.   Rails bent greatly. Underground pipelines completely out of service.

XII.   Damage nearly total. Large rock masses displaced. Lines of sight and level distorted. Objects thrown into the air.

---

larly useful for relief workers and those who have to plan for such emergencies. The absolute scale of earthquake magnitudes (the Richter Scale) compares with the Mercalli scale in the same way that absolute wind speeds compare to the Beaufort scale; the magnitude of the 1906 earthquake was $8 \cdot 3$, and as a rule of thumb for metropolitan centers in California the NOAA study team use the empirical relationship

$$\text{magnitude} = 1 + \tfrac{2}{3} \text{ intensity}$$

For the 1906 event this gives

$$\text{magnitude} = 1 + \tfrac{2}{3} \times 11 = 8 \cdot 33$$

On this basis, earthquakes of magnitude less than six (intensity of about VII or less) are expected to be dealt with by local communities. The 1971 San Fernando earthquake, which caused 58 deaths, 5000 injuries and damage worth nearly 500 million dollars, was of intensity VIII to IX, magnitude $6 \cdot 6$.

The worst event considered by the NOAA report is another earthquake of magnitude 8·3 occurring on the San Andreas fault near San Francisco. The length of faulting associated with this would be between 300 and 500 km, and displacement would occur by 6 m horizontally and 1·5 m vertically. The report considers many effects which are commonly forgotten in preparing for such disasters. For example, although almost everyone would realize the fire risk arising after an earthquake, city dwellers might well be unaware of the dangers of associated landslides. Because the report calculates maximum possible effects for all these associated problems, it is not possible simply to add up all the figures they quote to provide a typical picture of a San Francisco earthquake. Indeed, there is no such typical event because while fire hazard is greatest in the dry season, landslides will be more pronounced in the wet, and so on. But we can draw a thumbnail sketch of much of what can be expected to happen.

In 1971, one particular aspect of the San Fernando earthquake provided a grim reminder of one of the greatest problems facing survivors of a major earthquake in a densely populated region. Of fifty-eight deaths directly attributed to that earthquake, forty-one people died immediately in the collapse of the Veterans Hospital and six people injured in the collapse died later from their injuries. Shaking ground does not kill people but collapsing buildings do; and it is the old, sick and infirm who cannot move out of buildings when the ground begins to shake who are most likely to be seriously injured. Another important factor is the time of day on which the earthquake comes—during the rush hour, when everyone is asleep, or when people are at work. So the NOAA report calculates the results of disaster striking at 2.00 p.m., 4.30 p.m. and 2.30 a.m.

There are 85 major hospitals, with more than 36,-000 beds, in the San Francisco Bay area. Their facilities are valued at more than 1000 million dollars. For the earthquake of magnitude $8 \cdot 3$, centered on the San Francisco part of the San Andreas fault, the 2.00 p.m. and 4.30 p.m. timings give the same casualties in hospitals—nearly 1300 killed and 8000 injured. At 2.30 a.m. deaths would be about 425 and injuries over 3000. Doctors, patients, staff and visitors would all be numbered among the victims, just at the time when demands for medical aid would be pouring in from the stricken city, and 50 per cent of the hospital beds would be lost, together with vital medical supplies. The dollar loss could be as much as 70 per cent, although no one is likely to be counting dollars at the time. This, of course, is why the so-called Packaged Disaster Hospitals will be vital after the earthquake of 1982.

These portable hospitals (which were originally planned as Civil Defense Emergency Hospitals) do, however, require large vehicles to move them into the disaster area, and the total bed capacity they can provide in the Bay area will be only 7000 while something like 17,000 beds may have been lost in the damage to existing hospitals.

The pattern is repeated in the exhaustive study made by NOAA of other essential facilities. Fire services, ambulance services and so on are not adequate to cope with such a disaster, although hopefully the situation may improve slightly before 1982. But the greatest potential hazard of all lies in dam failure. This is when deaths climbing into tens of thousands (or even hundreds of thousands) can occur, and there are at least half a dozen dams in the Bay area which could be damaged by large enough shocks. Of these, the Calaveras, San Pablo and Upper San Leandro dams are least

likely to stand up to such shocks, according to the
NOAA report, and efforts are being made to improve
their safety.

Next to these problems, the risk to airports, public
buildings, port facilities and so on, important though
it is, can be no concern of ours. All we can do is encourage the authorities to take action in accordance
with reports such as the NOAA study of the Bay area
and a similar study of the expected impact of a major
earthquake on the Los Angeles area. Their task is not
to be envied—consider the problems facing our com-
puterized society when industry is trying to rebuild
with its computers and records destroyed—but they
must not be allowed to fall back into the complacency
of previous generations. And nor must individuals.

Official Preparations for Los Angeles
Area Earthquakes

In a report published in late 1973, the NOAA team
headed by Dr. S. T. Algermissen studied the extent
of an earthquake disaster in the Los Angeles area. The
report assumes that the worst possible quakes would be
of magnitude 8·3 on the San Andreas fault itself (simi·
lar to the 1857 Fort Tejon quake) or magnitude 7·6
on the Newport–Inglewood fault (similar to the 1933
Long Beach quake).

The length of ground rupture to be associated with
a major quake on the San Andreas north of Los Angeles would be 200-300 miles, with 7 m horizontal
and 1·5 m vertical displacement. The death toll predicted for such an 8·3 magnitude quake ranges from
3,000 to 12,000 people, depending on whether it occurred at 2 a.m. or 2 p.m. Similar casualty figures

would be expected for a 45-mile rupture along the Newport–Inglewood fault.

In the 1971 quake, the Lower San Fernando dam came very near to collapse. The danger of large ground accelerations and subsequent dam failures would enhance the casualty figures cited earlier. The projected quake on the San Andreas itself would make possible the failure of the Fairmont and Bouquet Canyon dams, with a subsequent inundation killing perhaps 9,000 people and rendering 110,000 people homeless. An earthquake along the Newport–Inglewood fault might collapse the Castonic and Pyramid Creek dams, with similar loss of life and destruction of homes.

The fracturing of water mains and subsequent failure of water supplies in the Los Angeles area as the result of a large earthquake poses two major threats. Health hazards are important, but more distressing is the threat of several major fires. Anyone familiar with the 1906 San Francisco quake knows that the greatest loss of life and property came from fire. An 8·3 magnitude San Andreas earthquake could generate three to four major fires, while an 7·6 magnitude quake could cause an even greater conflagration, including a major petroleum fire in the Terminal Island–Los Angeles Harbor area. The NOAA report notes that in the fall and winter, the Los Angeles area is blessed with a local meteorological phenomena known as "devil winds" or "Santa Anas"—hot dry winds that may reach 100 mph in the mountain passes; gusts up to 85 mph anywhere in the Greater Los Angeles are not uncommon. A "Santa Ana" occurring simultaneously with a major earthquake would greatly accelerate the extent of any fire. The NOAA report notes that under these conditions, a major fire storm in Los Angeles (e.g. Hamburg and Dresden in World War II) cannot be discounted.

Effect of Major California Earthquakes on Individuals

What can we expect, as individuals, when the earthquake does occur? The broad picture is all very well, but most people naturally want to know first what they can do to protect their homes and families. The only really safe course is to move out of San Francisco or Los Angeles, and live in a region of continuing creep activity, rather than the false calm of a stick-slip part of the fault—that is, if you must live near the fault at all. Secondly, take care not to live below a dam; this may sound facetious, but, incredibly, structures have actually been built across the fault line itself—with one wall riding the Pacific plate and the other anchored in the continental plate of North America. In the face of such deliberate blindness to the dangers, it seems that even the most simple precautions must be spelled out.

This failure to take appropriate precautions is all the more distressing because, with the understanding of geophysics spelled out in the early chapters of this book, it is possible to establish straightforward, easy rules to minimize damage. For the 1906 slip the fault zone moved significantly only over a band stretching roughly 300 m either side of the fault line and it would have been so easy even to leave this band clear in subsequent years. But that was not done.

One of the major snags about active fault regions from this point of view is that by and large they are associated with wide valleys which are visually very pleasing and thus encourage people to settle in them. Also, when geologists and geophysicists talk about the large-scale movements along the San Andreas fault in particular, people tend to dismiss this as something only important on a geological time scale, that is, over millions of years. It is probably too late to counter the results of this blasé attitude before the next great California earthquake. But by pointing out what has been done wrongly over the past seventy-odd years perhaps we can pave the way for a more suitable program of rebuilding and development next time.

Three kinds of damage result from the earthquakes, caused by the movement of the fault itself, associated shaking of the ground, and the breakup or failure of the ground. The first kind of damage need never occur if only mankind had enough sense not to build structures which cross the fault line—this is easy enough to see or to trace geologically throughout the regions at risk and anyone who has built a house or other construction across the edges of the two plates is simply a fool. There are, it seems, a lot of fools now living in California.

The damage caused by shaking is more of a problem. This depends on the kind of ground beneath the buildings at risk, their distance from the fault and the nature of their construction, as well, of course, as on the intensity of the earthquake itself. To some extent suitable construction can counter the effects of landsliding and other forms of ground failure, but here again the original siting of buildings is of the greatest importance. Even so a soundly constructed building resting on stable ground adjacent to the fault line is, comparatively speaking, less of a hazard than a badly engineered construction built on unsuitable ground even several miles from the fault line, although this is no excuse for indiscriminate building within the immediate fault zone.

During the earthquake of the early 1980s many unsuitably constructed buildings will be demolished for us. By and large those that remain will be the ones we can trust to withstand shocks. We must make sure that the rebuilding program results in the construction only of such buildings.

One of the best examples of intelligent planning is in the City of Fremont, where a Civic Center and shopping center have been built in the area of two fault traces associated with the San Andreas system. Movements along these traces occurred in 1836 and 1868, and the region is part of the area of activity not associated with the greatest earthquakes. Even so, thoughtless construction could result in large-scale losses during even small earthquakes. But in these developments the city authorities have planned parking lots and other open spaces for the areas crossed by the faults, with all buildings set to one side or the other. Since buildings are pretty much at the same risk there or several miles away, this is making the best of a bad job.

So there are two extremes which might occur in building development near the San Andreas fault. Indiscriminate building, with structures even straddling the fault, or planning which allows only parks and other open spaces for a certain area around. As always there is bound to be a compromise in practice, although we may hope that never again will the compromise be weighted so heavily in favor of the 'build anywhere and be damned' approach. This applies equally to active regions of the fault as to the temporarily locked lengths which can be triggered into major earthquake activity. Along most of the fault system virtually all earthquake damage can be avoided by building restrictions within 30 m or so of the fault line. Is that so much to ask? And yet in the San Francisco

Peninsula, where memories of 1906 should prompt some caution, lines of so-called sag ponds, which geologists use as a clear indicator of the fault line, have been filled in to make building land!

There are two ways in which the problem might be resolved. Perhaps the civil authorities will belatedly grasp the nettle, taking action to rehouse inhabitants of danger zones and make long green belts of danger areas not yet developed. This seems unlikely because by the time the State of California can gear itself up to such action, even if it began now, the next earthquake will have occurred. In that case there must surely be sensible planning afterwards. Otherwise as knowledge of the workings of the San Andreas fault spreads there will probably be an increase in insurance premiums within the narrow highest-risk zones. Within two years of 1982 (between 1980 and 1984) there will be a major disaster, probably in the Los Angeles area but perhaps in the San Francisco Bay area. This, together with further increases in insurance, will encourage industry and individuals to move out of the fault zone throughout the state, regardless of government action or inaction. Property values will drop and safety zones will grow up anyway, because the crippling insurance rates will make the danger regions uneconomic to live in. The wise will not wait so long, but will move at once.

Since the great San Francisco earthquake of 1906 the dangers of the San Andreas fault system have been clear. But in spite of this the population of California, and especially of the two great cities of Los Angeles and San Francisco, has grown apace. Lured by the many advantages of the state, most people turned a blind eye to the dangers. Only a few geologists worried about the prospect of another great earthquake, but they could attract little attention when they could not explain the cause of such disasters, let alone where they might occur. Over the past few years all that has changed. The new, developing understanding of the forces which shape the Earth has led geophysicists to construct a picture in which the continents ride on great plates of solid rock, floating on molten rock of the Earth's interior. The plates jostle against one another as they move, and the San Andreas fault defines the boundary between two such plates. At the same time, geologists at last began to understand what happens to rock subjected to the kind of forces which arise at these plate boundaries.

It must be emphasized again that not every earthquake along the San Andreas fault or elsewhere in the world is triggered by the tides acting either directly or indirectly through solar activity and the intermediaries of the weather and changes in the Earth's rotation. Many earthquakes, as we pointed out earlier in this chapter, occur in regions where creep is important or where the local geology precludes changes in the pore pressure in the rocks. The prediction of a large earthquake in California in 1982 does not mean that similar quakes, triggered by the same mechanism, cannot occur elsewhere, say along the very active Anatolian fault in the Middle East. For obvious reasons, we have chosen to study California in detail; anyone else doing so for other areas along the margins of tectonic plates may arrive at similar conclusions to our own.

Geologists can now explain how strain accumulates in the faults, and why it is released in great surges like the San Francisco earthquake of 1906 and the Los Angeles earthquake of 1857. They can even pin down the most dangerous regions of the fault—today, the prime area of risk is around Los Angeles, with San Francisco, the 'City that Waits to Die' as it has been called, only the secondary danger zone. All that remains is to predict when the next disaster will occur. Today, people are at last aware of the danger, and the most straightforward indicator, that great earthquakes occur in California every half-century, hints to everyone, not just geophysicists, that the day of reckoning cannot be far away.

Now we can predict this apocalyptic date to within a couple of years. A remarkable chain of evidence, much of it known for decades but never before linked together, points to 1982 as the year in which the Los Angeles region of the San Andreas fault will be subjected to the most massive earthquake known in the populated regions of the Earth in this century. At the end point of the chain, directly causing this disaster, is a rare alignment of the planets in the Solar System. By disturbing the equilibrium of the Sun, which in turn disturbs the whole Earth, the planets can trigger earthquakes. The trail links astrology—for that is really what the study of planetary alignments is, even though we can explain their effects in sound scientific terms—astronomy, meteorology, geology, geophysics and other sciences. Small wonder that pieces of this chain have lain about unrecognized for so long. But now they have been put together there is no question about the implication: in 1982 'when the Moon is in the Seventh House, and Jupiter aligns with Mars' and with the other seven planets of the Solar System, Los Angeles will be destroyed. The astrological link with the dawning of the age of Aquarius may or may not be coincidence; that is outside the scope of this book, which contains only solid scientific evidence and reasoning.

Appendix A
Recent Developments in Earthquake Prediction

Geophysics is still a rapidly developing subject, and now that the basic concept of plate tectonics has become firmly established, increasing attention is being paid to using the new geophysical knowledge in practical ways. One of the most important lines of present geophysical research concerns earthquake prediction, and even while this book was being written important developments were made in that area. In particular, one aspect of research that gained widespread publicity in 1973 seems to offer a mechanism to account for another link in the chain we have forged tying earthquakes to planetary alignments—and makes practical use of the knowledge gained from the 'lubrication' experiments (see chapter 4).

But although the story became widely known in 1973, it actually goes back for several years. Soviet scientists were, it seems, the first to discover a reliable premonitory indicator of one particular kind of earthquake. Experimenters in the Garm area of the Soviet Union were monitoring regularly many possible geophysical indicators, such as electrical resistance of rocks and water levels in wells, in the hope that one or more of these factors might prove to vary in some clear way shortly before earthquakes. And they struck lucky. One property in particular, the velocity of sound waves through the rocks (the seismic velocity) does indeed change noticeably before an earthquake.

The Soviet geophysicists found that several days before an earthquake the ratio of the velocities through the rock of two kinds of waves—shear waves and compressional waves—changes by as much as 20 per cent of its value. Immediately before the earthquake the velocity ratio returns to normal. This exciting news would probably have been quickly publicized in the West, since it offers the exciting prospect first of being able to say that an earthquake is due fairly soon, then, when the velocity ratio returns to normal, of being able to say that the earthquake is imminent. But it was not until similar studies were carried out in upstate New York by a team from the Lamont–Doherty Observatory that this new tool for predicting earthquakes became generally known.

The American work confirmed the Soviet studies, and provided the publicity impetus needed for the further development of the prediction tool. For of course this first discovery was not a great deal of use in itself. Although it is easy enough to measure the velocity ratio which is the key to these predictions, that can only be done if some disturbance has produced shock waves to measure. That is why upstate New York is a handy place to study seismic velocities—the area is prone to repeated, very small earthquakes. But as we have seen in this book, areas where repeated small disturbances occur are those where strain cannot accumulate; the really dangerous areas are those like the locked portions of the San Andreas fault, where no small earthquakes are available for constant monitoring of seismic velocities.

How could this problem be resolved? Not by setting off explosive charges throughout regions suspected of being in a state of strain in order to measure the resulting shock waves, since quite apart from the inconvenience to inhabitants and the enormous cost, most scientists today are extremely cautious about tampering with forces as ill understood as those which produce earthquakes. It would hardly have gone down well with inhabitants of Los Angeles, say, if a moderate earthquake had occurred soon after geophysicists had fired a series of test explosions in deep boreholes. So the seismologists turned to another technique, and tried to measure the seismic velocities in rocks near their monitoring stations by studying shock waves coming from moderately large earthquakes halfway around the world. The jackpot came as recently as 21 September 1973, with a report published in *Nature* describing the results of an analysis of Japanese records made ten years before.

In the early 1960s the Japanese seismologists who made recordings of seismic velocities had no way of knowing how useful their work would prove. But it turns out that their records of shock waves from earthquakes nowhere near Japan do provide a measure of the changing seismic velocities in the rocks near their monitoring station. And the critical velocity ratio changed before a major earthquake in just the same way that the velocities in Garm and New York had been seen to change before lesser earthquakes.

With this new-found wealth of data, geophysicists have been able to make new strides in developing the velocity test as an earthquake predictor. It turns out that the length of time for which the velocity ratio remains depressed below its usual value reveals the approximate size of the earthquake to come. Perhaps we are not too far from the day when routine monitoring stations will be able to tell us first that an earthquake is on the way, then, as the days, weeks or months go by and the velocity ratio remains low, roughly how big the earthquake will be if it comes next week, and finally, after the velocity ratio returns to normal, that the quake is indeed coming next week.

How do the lubrication experiments tie in with this? It seems that the best explanation for the curious changes in seismic velocities is that as strain builds up in water-saturated rocks a point is reached where cracks open up in the rock faster than fluid can flow in to fill them. In rock not saturated with water the ratio of seismic velocities is lower than in saturated rock, as is shown by laboratory tests. Just before the earthquake no more cracks are being formed but water is flowing into the now unsaturated rock, increasing the pore pressure and the vital velocity ratio. Finally the earthquake occurs through a lubrication-aided process similar to those of the recent experimentally induced earthquakes.

So a fairly short-term warning of earthquakes is now practicable in regions where seismic velocities are monitored; commenting on this, and in particular the study of Japanese records, Dr. David Davies, the editor of *Nature* and himself a seismologist, said in September 1973 that it shows 'there are still good things in existing geophysical data for those who can look for them with a new eye'. Looking back on this book, in which all we have done is to gather in one volume data from scattered sources and look at them anew, we are tempted to say that Dr. Davies's comment applies not just to geophysics but to the whole of science.

Appendix B
Our Weather: a Link with the Planets?

One of the most important links in the chain we have discovered tieing planetary alignments to earthquake activity is formed by the influence of the Sun on the Earth's atmosphere. In the latter part of 1973, there has been a resurgence of interest in the way solar activity affects weather and climate; it seems that in the months to come there is a very real prospect that this part of the chain will become even better understood, as a result of research going on around the world. The importance now attached to these studies was highlighted when NASA and the University Corporation for Atmospheric Research and the American Meteorological Society jointly sponsored a conference on 'Possible Relationships between Solar Activity and Meteorological Phenomena' in November, 1973. And the immediate relevance of this kind of work to the problems we have looked at in this book is shown in the following article by one of us (J.G.), reprinted from New Scientist, volume 60, p. 893, December 27, 1973:

The past year has seen an explosive growth of interest in climatic change. This work is timely in view of the famine belt now afflicting people along the southern edges of northern hemisphere deserts. Though it will be some years before climatic research produces use-

ful results, a curious and near-astrological possibility
has already emerged—namely that the planets, by influencing the Sun tidally, can affect the Earth's weather.

The events of recent months in the sub-Sahara region of Africa, in Ethiopia, and in India have highlighted the need for some form of climatic prediction
if human suffering on a disastrous scale is not to be
caused by further unexpected failures of the rainfall on
which crops depend. Over the years many people have
investigated the question of predicting the way our
climate might change, but until recently this kind of
work had a slight underground flavor. The publicity
associated with recent droughts has brought the problem to the public mind. But climatic research was already making great strides towards professional re-
spectability both because of the development of better
systems for measuring what goes on in the atmosphere
(from satellites, for example), and because the computer facilities needed to produce useful models of atmospheric circulation are just becoming available. At
the same time the collection of historical and other evidence into a coherent whole (notably by the Climatic
Research Unit at East Anglia University) has provided
a firm basis against which to assess theories of climatic
change.

Patterns of climatic change

The right theory, or theories, will not emerge over-
night. It is already becoming clear, however, that some
of the ideas which have been around, and largely ignored, in the past, have more than a grain of truth in
them. At the same time, there are now theories which
look very hopeful, and which make concrete predictions about the immediate climatic future, so that they

can be tested simply by waiting for a couple of decades. Perhaps inevitably, the most exciting ideas are those which link meteorological changes to other phenomena affecting the whole Earth-system; one line of approach which looks particularly promising, and has been tackled intermittently at least since the 1950s, is the evidence of a link between the Earth's magnetism and climate. This idea surfaced once again in 1973, when a team from the Lamont–Doherty Geological Observatory showed that magnetic and climatic changes have followed parallel courses during this century (*Nature,* vol. 242, p. 34); decreasing magnetism, in general, relates to a warming climate (like that in the present day northern hemisphere) and vice versa. As the Lamont team said, 'a close relationship links changes in the Earth's magnetic field and climate,' and they went on to suggest that both effects may be the result of varying solar activity.

That suggestion looks increasingly plausible as ideas about climatic change have developed in recent months. But before seeking the cause, perhaps it is appropriate to look a little more closely at the pattern of climatic change which is now affecting the world. Dr. Derek Winstanley, a London meteorologist, produced evidence in two papers in *Nature* (vol. 243, p. 464 and vol. 245, p. 190) of a pattern of climatic change taking place over the whole northern hemisphere. The key evidence he provided can be summed up in two graphs (figures 1 and 2). The first shows a decline in rainfall over recent years throughout the regions now affected by serious drought; without more data, the graph cannot be extrapolated with confidence, and for all we know could now have bottomed out. Figure 2 shows the concomitant increase in rainfall further north, as the temperate rain belt has, apparently, shifted bodily southwards during these years. The clue to a cause of the change—or at least, another link in the casual chain—comes from the second line in figure 2. This reveals a very clear anti-correlation between the changes in winter/spring rainfall and the mean altitude of the 500-millibar surface along 40°N. The decrease in altitude of this surface during the 1960s signifies 'an increase in the southward extent of the troughs in the circumpolar westerlies', says Winstanley. This pattern of change also explains the very high rainfalls recorded over large areas of North Africa and the Middle East in the late 1960s. In crude terms, the whole pattern of climatic zones in the northern atmosphere is shifting south; the northern Sahara, for example, is becoming correspondingly less arid even as the desert advances in the south. Even further north the same overall pattern suggests that Britain is in for drier summers in the coming years.

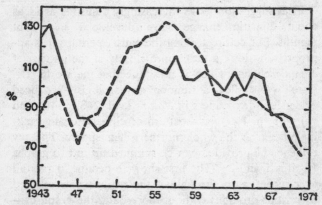

FIGURE 1. The percentage change in normal seasonal rainfall, expressed as five-year running means over recent years, for stations in north-west India and the Sudan (solid line); and for others in Mauritania, Mali and Niger (dotted line). Both show a decreasing trend from about 1956 onwards.

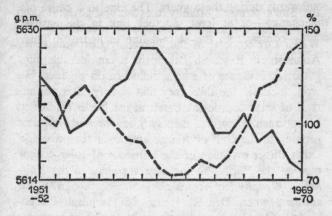

FIGURE 2. The percentage change in normal seasonal rainfall (dashed line) for stations in India, Iran, Iraq, Lebanon, Israel, Saudi Arabia, Libya, Morocco and Mauritania shows a pronounced anticorrelation with the mean altitude (solid line) of the 500-mbar surface along latitude 40°N, between longitudes 110°W and 70°E. Data apply for the period October to May (Figures 1 and 2 from D. Winstanely, *Nature*, vol. 245, p. 190.)

Links with solar activity

So the specific climatic changes now going on most obviously in the drought-hit areas of the northern hemisphere can be related to at least hemispheric, and probably global, changes in climate. What sort of influence, either apart from, or perhaps as well as, the Earth's magnetic field, could affect the whole atmosphere in this way? The obvious candidate is the Sun. Solar heating, of course, provides the driving energy for the whole atmospheric circulation system, and climatologists have suggested that relatively minor changes in the Sun's output could be the cause of ice ages. But the changes going on now are on a smaller scale yet, in the Sun's terms. Certainly the Sun's slightest hiccup does affect the Earth's atmosphere measurably. Dr. Walter Orr Roberts of the University Corporation for Atmospheric Research has spent a considerable time gathering evidence of a solar influence on weather. His work includes the discovery that shortly after the arrival of solar cosmic-ray bursts at the Earth (indicated by spectacular auroral displays) low-pressure systems forming in the Gulf of Alaska are larger than average. Other direct evidence of the influence of solar cosmic rays on the Earth's atmosphere appeared in the *Journal of Geophysical Research* (vol. 78, p. 6167) this autumn, when Dr. R. Reiter of Garmisch–Partenkirchen, W. Germany, reported the results of monitoring the content of the radionuclides beryllium–7 and phosphorus–32 in the atmosphere at the top of the Zugspitze, three km above sea level in the Bavarian Alps. Sharp increases in the levels of these nuclides indicate the injection of stratospheric air down into the lower troposphere. Reiter has found that such increases can be closely correlated with the arrival of solar cosmic and X-rays (monitored by probes such as Explorer 35) at the top of the atmosphere.

These observations, and those of Roberts, are particularly important because of the difficulties theoreticians have in producing plausible mechanisms coupling solar and meteorological activity. As Dr. A. J. Dessler, of Rice University, pointed out at a recent symposium at NASA's Goddard Spaceflight Center in Maryland, the sun produces 10^6 ergs/sq. cm/s, but the energy available to the atmosphere of the Earth from the solar wind and interplanetary magnetic field is less than one millionth of that under normal conditions. Brute force is thus not enough to drive the observed meteorological response to solar flares, and some 'trigger mechanism' must be proposed. Trigger mechanisms are usually the theoretician's last resort; while it is true that they definitely work sometimes (in the way that a snowball released at the top of a mountain can cause an avalanche) they do need some available energy source to tap. But with evidence of the kind found by Roberts in Alaska and Reiter in Bavaria, it cannot be denied that the Sun does affect the weather; nor (since brute force won't work) can it be denied that, unpalatable though it may be, a trigger mechanism of some kind must provide the necessary link.

Those observations and arguments apply to specific events on the Sun—solar flares and the cosmic-ray bursts that they produce. Now another old idea which used to be frowned upon as rather cranky has re-emerged, looking much stronger than ever before Dr. J. W. King, of the Appleton Laboratory, has put together a lot of evidence which has been around for many years and suggests that variations and trends in the Earth's climate over decades are associated with solar variations over the 11-year sunspot cycle (*Nature,* vol. 245, p. 443). Professor H. H. Lamb has summarized attempts to relate solar cycles to climatic change in his book *Climate Present, Past and Future* (Methuen, 1968) and as King is the first to point out, these ideas are not new, just little known. The evidence comes from many diverse and wondrous sources. They include conventional meteorological records; careful interpretation of the statistics in Wisden to find good summers during the nineteenth century; and (one not mentioned by King) astronomical folklore like the common story that more comets are observed at certain phases of the sunspot cycle. Assuming that comets are not attracted by sunspots, it is plausible to suggest that more are observed at sunspot maximum because the weather is better then, and the skies are free from obscuring cloud. But King does more than suggest that climatic variations relate to solar changes over one solar cycle; as figure 3 shows, the average activity of the Sun over a whole cycle seems to be related to important, practical, meteorological effects on Earth.

Predicting the changes

These considerations augur very well for climate prediction—all we have to do apparently, is work out the future pattern of solar sunspot activity and voilà! climate prediction becomes a reality. Unfortunately, sunspots are among the most baffling phenomena within 100 million miles of Earth. It would take a very brave man to predict how the average 'strength' of future sunspot cycles will compare to those of the past. Fortunately, there are such brave men around. Just over a year ago Professor K. D. Wood, of the University of Colorado, suggested a method of sunspot prediction based on the influence of the 'tidal planets'—Mercury, Venus, Earth and Jupiter—on the Sun (*Nature,* vol. 240, p. 91). Only these four planets produce significant tides on the Sun's surface, the first three because they are close to the Sun, and Jupiter because it is so big.

The exact magnitude of the combined tide can be calculated for any time during which sunspots have been observed. Wood found that there is a close link between the time of greatest tide on the Sun and the time of sunspot maximum; there is also a less precise link between the height of the tide at maximum and the maximum number of sunspots in the associated cycle.

At first sight, this result looks decidedly odd. How

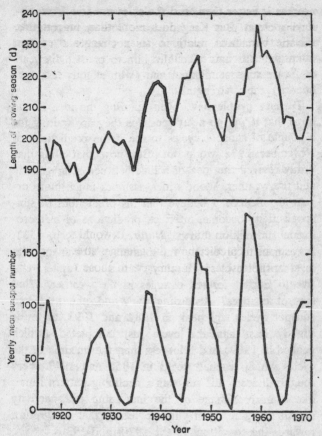

FIGURE 3. Changes in the length of the 'growing season' (a) at Eskdalemuir correlate strikingly with the yearly sunspot number (b). (From J. W. King, *Nature*, vol. 245, p. 443.)

can the small tidal effect of these planets influence the sunspot cycle (or perhaps even cause the sunspot cycle)? The best theories (not perfect, but the best we have) say that sunspots are very much a magnetic phenomenon, and how would the tides affect that?

Another trigger mechanism? So, even though Wood's data are very clear cut, and leave little or no room for other explanations, his idea has not received a lot of attention, although it enables him to predict the years of future sunspot maxima and (with slightly less confidence) their 'strength'.

Perhaps people have been ignoring the idea in the hope that it will go away; perhaps they are waiting for a couple of sunspot cycles to see if the predictions of November 1972 work out. But now that King has firmly revived the idea of a link between solar activity and the weather, Wood's idea assumes much more urgent significance. I believe that his predictions of sunspot activity become, in effect, predictions of meteorological activity on Earth (*Nature*, vol. 246, p. 453). In astronomical terms, the planetary alignments (at least in the cases of Mercury, Venus and Jupiter relative to Earth) foretell changes in the weather. What sort of changes? According to Wood, the next two sunspot cycles will peak in 1982 and 1993, at levels slightly less than the cycle just completed (which peaked in 1969) and a lot less than the maxima of the cycles which reached peaks in 1958 and 1947. Very roughly indeed, this suggests a declining pattern rather like a mirror image of the increasing peak activity shown in figure 3; in climatic terms, that is a return towards the conditions of the 1920s and 1930s.

However, this interpretation is very simple-minded. It takes no account of other related and unrelated processes, and it should not be accepted too seriously. What should be taken seriously by meteorologists is the possibility of using Wood's predictions of solar activity in conjunction with other methods being developed to predict future climatic trends. The ideas may not be quite rounded off, and they may still smack of underground associations with astrology; but if there is any chance that they may help to save lives they should not be ignored.

Further Reading

The headings preceding each section of this list of further reading do not refer to chapters but to the general areas covered by this book. We hope that they will be of use to anyone who wants to look further into the problems of earthquakes and related phenomena.

Plate Tectonics and the Early History of the California Fault System

Anderson, D. L. The San Andreas Fault, *Scientific American* (November 1971)

Calder, N. *The Restless Earth,* Viking Press (1972)

Danby, T. Y. California's San Andreas Fault, *National Geographic* (January 1973)

Smith, P. J. *Topics in Geophysics,* Open University Press (1973); MIT Press (1973)

Wallace, R. E. Earthquake Recurrence Intervals on the San Andreas Fault, *Bull. Geol. Soc. Am.,* **81** (1970), 2875

Wood, H. O. The 1857 Earthquake in California, *Bull. Seis. Soc. Am.,* **45** (1955), 47

Understanding the Earth, MIT Press (1971)

Detailed Geology of the San Andreas Fault System

Allen, C. R. Relation between Seismicity and Geologic Structure in the Southern California Region, *Bull. Seis. Soc. Am.,* **55** (1965), 753

Benioff, H. Seismic Evidence for Crustal Structure and Tectonic Activity, *Geol. Soc. Am. Spec. Paper 62*, p. 61 (1955)

Dickinson, W. R. and Grantz, A. (eds.) *Proceed. Conf. in Geologic Problems of San Andreas Fault System*, 11, Stanford Univ. Publ., Stanford, Calif. (1968)

McKenzie, D. P. Plate Tectonics, in *The Nature of the Solid Earth* (ed. E. C. Robertson), McGraw–Hill Book Co., New York (1972), p. 323

Savage, J. C. and Burford, R. D. Accumulation of Tectonic Strain in California, *Bull. Sers. Soc. Am.* **60** (1970), 1877

Strain in Rocks and Fracturing Experiments in the Laboratory

Byerlee, J. D. and Brace, W. F. Stick Slip, Stable Sliding, and Earthquakes, *J. Geophys. Res.*, **73** (1968), 6031

Robertson, E. C. Strength of Metamorphosed Graywacke and Other Rocks, in *The Nature of the Solid Earth*, McGraw–Hill Book Co., New York (1972), p. 631

Robertson, E. C. Viscoelasticity, in *State of Stress in the Earth's Crust* (ed. W. R. Judd), Elsevier Pub. Co., New York (1964), p. 31

Weertman, J. The Creep Strength of the Earth's Mantle, *Rev. Geophys. & Sp. Phys.*, **8** (1970), 145; *Nature Phys. Sci.* **231** (1971), 9

Earthquakes, the Weather and Changes in the Earth's Rotation

Anderson, D. Earthquakes and the Rotation of the Earth, *Science,* **186** (1974), 49.

Challinor, R. A. Variations in the Rate of Rotation of the Earth, *Science* **172** (1971), 1022

Dahlen, F. A. The excitation of the Chandler Wobble by earthquake, *Geophys., J.,* **25** (1971), 157

Goldreich, P. and Toomre, A. Some Remarks on Polar Wandering, *F. Geophys. Res.,* **74** (1969), 2555

Mansinha, L. and Smylie, D. E. Seismic Excitation of the Chandler Wobble, in *Earthquake Displacement Fields and the Rotation of the Earth,* Reidel, Holland (1970), p. 122

Melchoir, P. *Rotation of the Earth,* D. Reidel Pub. Co., Holland (1972)

Mintz, Y. and Munk, W. H. The Effect of Winds and Tides on the Length of the Day, *Tellus,* **3** (1951), 117; *Geophys. Supp. Mon. Not. Roy. Astr. Soc.,* **6** (1954), 566

Munk, W. H. and Macdonald, G. J. F. *The Rotation of the Earth,* Cambridge University Press (1960).

Pines, D. and Shaham, J. Seismic Activity, Polar Tides and the Chandler Wobble, *Nature,* **245** (1973), 77

Van Den Dungen, F. H., *et al.* Sur la periode annuelle de la fréquence des seismes, *Bull. Roy. Belg. Acad.,* **37** (1951), 1037, **38** (1952), 607

Vidorenkov, N. S. The Influence of Atmosphere Circulation on the Earth's Rotational Velocity, *Soviet Astronomy AJ,* **12** (1968), pp. 303 and 706

Do Earth Tides Trigger Quakes?

Corrandi, R. A. The Variation of Earth Tides as a Triggering Mechanism in Earthquakes, NTIS Report AD-769758 (1973)

Filson, J., Simkin, T., and Leu, L. Seismicity of a Caldera Collapse: Galapagos Islands 1968, *J. Geophys. Res.,* **78** (1973), 8591

George, W. O. and Romberg, F. E. Tide-Producing

Forces and Artesian Pressures, *Trans. Am. Geophys. Union,* **32** (1951) 369

Latham, G., *et al.* Moonquakes, *Science,* **174,** (1971) 687; see also *Science* **181** (1973) 49; The Moon, **7** (1973), 396

Melchoir, P. *The Earth Tides,* Pergamon Press, New York (1966)

Myerson, R. J. Evidence for Association of Earthquakes with the Chandler Wobble, Using Long Term Polar Data of the ILS–IPMS, in *Earthquakes, Displacement Fields and the Rotation of the Earth (eds. Mansinha, Smylie and Beck),* Reidel, Holland (1970) p. 159

Pariyski, N. N., et al. On the Problem of the Role of Trigger Mechanism in Earthquakes, *Akad.* Nauk USSR-Inst. *Geophys.* (1970) 62

Ryall, A., *et al.* Triggering of Microearthquakes by Earth Tides, *Bull. Seis. Soc. Am.* **58** (1968) 215

Slichter, L. B. Earth Tides, in *The Nature of the Solid Earth* (ed. E. C. Robertson), McGraw–Hill Book Co., New York (1972) p. 285

Shaw, H. R. Earth Tides, Global Heat Flow, and Tectonics, *Science,* **168** (1970) 1084; *Bull. Geol. Soc. Am.,* **82** (1971) 869; Scale Effects in the Study of Earth Tides, *Journal of Rheology* (1974)

Shlien, S. Earthquake-Tide Correlation, *Geophys. F. Roy. Astr. Soc.,* **28** (1972) 27

Tamrazyan, G. P. Tides and Earthquakes, *Icarus,* **7** (1967) 59; see also *J. Geophys. Res.,* **73** (1968) 6013

How Solar Flares and Cosmic Rays Effect the Earth's Spin

Coffey, H. E. *Collected Data Reports on August 1972 Solar Terrestrial Events,* NOAA Report UAG–28 (1973)

Danjon, A. Solar Flares and Changes in the Length of the Day, *C. R. Acad. Sci. Ser. B.,* **249** (1959) 2254; *Ibid.,* **250** (1960) 1399; *Ibid.,* **252** (1961) 2779

Druzhinin, I. P. and Khamyaova, N. V., Solar Activity and Sudden Changes in the Natural Processes on Earth—A Statistical Analysis, Translation from a Russian monograph by NASA (1974) TTF-652 (NTIS document TT 70-57264).

Gribbin, J. and Plagemann, S. Discontinuous Change in Earth's Spin following Great Solar Storm of August 1972, *Nature,* **243** (1973) 26

Hirshberg, J. Upper Limit of the Torque of the Solar Wind on the Earth, *J. Geophys. Res.,* **77** (1972) 4855

McKinnon, J. A. *August 1972 Solar Activity and Related Geophysical Effects,* NOAA Tech. Mem. ERLMSEL–22 (1972)

Rosenberg, R. L. and Coleman, P. J. Heliographic Latitude Dependence of the Dominant Polarity of the Interplanetary Magnetic Field, *J. Geophys. Res.,* **74** (1969) 5611

Shatzman, E. Interplanetary Torques, in *The Earth Moon System* (eds. Cameron, A. G. W., and Marsden, B. G.), Plenum Press, New York (1966) p. 12

Sugawa, C., *et al.* On the Relation between the Rotation of the Earth and Solar Activity, *Pub. Int. Latitude Obs. of Mizusawa, Japan,* **8** (1972) 105

Wilcox, J. M. The Interplanetary Magnetic Field, Solar Origin and Terrestrial Effects, *Sp. Sci. Rev.,* **8** (1968) 258

Wilcox, J. M. and Ness, N. F. *Geophys. Res.* **70** (1965) 5793

The Physical Links of the Sun and the Earth

Abbot, C. G. *Smithsonian Misc. Collections,* 448 (1966) 7

Brier, G. W. Diurnal and Semidiurnal Atmospheric Tides in Relation to Precipitation Variations, *Mon. Weath. Rev.,* **93** (1965) 93

Dessler, A. J. Some Problems in Coupling Solar Activity to Meteorological Phenomena, *Proceedings of Symposium on Solar Activity and the Weather,* Goddard Space Flight Center, Greenbelt, Maryland (1973)

Duell, B. and Duell, G. The Behaviour of Barometric Pressure During and After Solar Particle Invasions and Solar Ultraviolet Invasions, *Smithsonian Misc. Coll.,* **110** (1948) 8

Fritts, H. C. Dendroclimatology and Dendroecology, *Quarternary Research* **1** (1971) 419; *J. Appl. Meteorology,* **100** (1971) 845

Gribbin, J. Planetary alignments, Solar activity and climatic change, *Nature,* **246** (1973)

Hide, R. and Malin, S. R. C. Novel Correlations between Global Features of the Earth's Gravitational and Magnetic Fields, *Nature* **225** (1970) 605

Hines, C. O. Two Possible Mechanisms for Relating Terrestrial Atmospheric Circulation to Solar Disturbances, *Proc. Sympom. Solar Activity and Meteorological Phen.,* Goddard Space Flight Center (November 1973)

King, J. W. Solar Radiation Changes and the Weather, *Nature,* **245** (1973) 443; *Nature,* **274** (1974) 131

Kondratyev, K. Y. and Nikolsky, G. A. Solar Radiation and Solar Activity, *Q. Jl. Roy. Met. Soc.,* 96 (1970) 509

Macdonald, N. J. and Ward, F. The Prediction of

Geomagnetic Disturbance Indices, *J. Geophys. Res.*, **68** (1963) 3351

Mustel, E. R. *On the Reality of the Influence of Solar Corpuscular Streams upon the Lower Layer of the Earth's Atmosphere,* Publication No. 24, Astronomical Council, USSR Acad. of Sciences, Moscow (1972)

Roberts, W. O. and Olson, R. H. Geomagnetic Storms and Wintertime 300–mb Trough Development in the North Pacific–North Atlantic Area, *J. Atmos. Sci.* **30** (1973) 135; *Science* **180** (1973) 185; *Rev. Geophysics & Sp. Phys.,* **11** (1973) 731

Rosenberg, R. L. and Colman, P. J. 27-day cycle in the rainfall at Los Angeles, *Science* **250** (1974) 481

Schneider, S. H. and Mass, C. Volcanic Dust, Sunspots and Temperature Trends, *Science* **190** (1975) 741

Shapiro, R. Evidence of a Solar-Weather Effect, *J. Meteor* **13** (1956) 335; *J. Atm. Sci.,* **29** (1972) 1213

Wilcox, J. M. *Solar Activity and the Weather,* Stanford University Institute for Plasma Research, Report No. 544 (October 1973)

Willett, H. C. Long-Period Fluctuations of the General Circulation of the Atmosphere, *J. Meteor,* **6** (1948) 34

Zatopek, A. and Křivský, L. On the Correlation Between Meteorological Microseisms and Solar Activity, *Bull. Astron. Inst. Czech.,* **25** (1974), 257

The Solar Sunspot Cycle and the Alignment of the Planets

Bigg, E. K. Influence of the Planet Mercury on Sunspots, *Astronomical Journal*, **72** (1967) 463

Blizard, J. B. Long Range Solar Flare Prediction, NASA Contractor Report CR–61316 (1969), *Astron. J.*, **70** (1965) 677; *Bull. Am. Phys. Soc.*, **13** (June 1968)

Bureau, R. A. and Craine, L. B. Sunspots and Planetary Orbits, *Nature* **228** (1970), 984

Cohen, T. J. and Lintz, P. R. Long Term Periodicities in the Sunspot Cycle, *Nature* **250** (1974), 398

Dauvillier, A. Sur la Rotation Differentielle des Corps Celestes, *Bull. Roy. Soc. Liège*, **39** (1970) 486 (see also *Comp. Rendu.*, **2708** (1970) 1121

Jose, P. D. Sun's Motion and Sunspots, *Astron. J.*, **70** (1965) 193

Malburet, J. *Astronomie*, **39** (1925) 505

Meeus, J. Comments on 'The Jupiter Effect', *Icarus*, 26 (1975) 257; for our response, *Ibid.*, p. 268

Molchanov, A. M. The Resonant Structure of the Solar System, *Icarus* **8** (1968) 203; **11** (1969), pp. 95 and 104

Nelson, J. H. Circuit Reliability, Frequency Utilization, and Forecasting in the High Frequency Communications Band, in *The Effect of Disturbances of Solar Origin on Communications* (ed. G. J. Gassman), Macmillan, New York (1963) p. 293; *RCA Review*, (March 1951) 26; *Trans. IRE CS–2*, No. 1 (1954) 19

Okal, E. and Anderson, D. L. On the Planetary Theory of Sunspots, *Nature*, **253** (1975) 511

Opik, E. Planetary Tides and Sunspots, *Irish Astronomical Journal*, **10** (1972), 298

Sleeper, H. P. Planetary Resonances, Bi-Stable Oscillation Modes, and Solar Activity Cycles, *NASA Contractor Report CR–2035* (1972); "A Spectral Solar-Climatic Model," *Proc. Sympos. Solar Activity and*

Meteorological Phen., Goddard Space Flight Center (November 1973)

Takahashi, K. On the Relation between the Solar Activity Cycle and the Solar Tidal Force Induced by the Planets, *Solar Physics,* **3** (1968) 598

Shuvalov, V. M. Dependence of the Solar Cycle on the Positions of the Planets, *Astron. Vestnik,* **4** (1970), 198

Williams, D. Sunspot Cycle Correlations, Ann. NY Acad. Sci., **95** (1961) 78

Wood, K. D. Sunspots and Planets, *Nature* **240** (1972) 91; see also *Nature,* **208** (1965) 129

Wood, R. M. Comparison of Sunspot Periods with Planetary Synodic Period Resonances, *Nature,* **255** (1975) 312

Preparation for the Next Great California Earthquake

Algermissen, S. T., *et al. A Study of Earthquake Losses in the San Francisco Bay Area.* A Report Prepared for the Office of Emergency Preparedness by the National Oceanic and Atmospheric Administration, U.S. Dept. of Commerce (1972)

Algermissen, S. T., *et al. A Study of Earthquake Losses in the Los Angeles, California Bay Area.* A Report Prepared by NOAA for the Federal Disaster Relief Administration (1973)

Pakiser, L. C., *et al.* Earthquake Prediction and Control, *Science,* **166** (1969) 1467

Smith, P. J. Earthquakes Predicated, *Nature* **252** (1974), 9

Whitcomb, J. H., *et al.* Earthquake Prediction, *Science* **180** (1973) 632

Afterword

Since the original edition of this book appeared, the question we have been asked most often is, "What happened to the San Andreas fault 179 years *before* 1982, the last time the planets of the Solar System were all aligned on the same side of the Sun?" This question was rather embarrassing, since we could only give vague answers. At the beginning of the nineteenth century California was only sparsely populated, and no detailed records of earthquakes were kept. In addition, we have no way of knowing for sure whether or not any part of the San Andreas was in a state of tension comparable to that it is in today (in the southern part, at least). And, as we have stressed throughout this book, our planetary/solar hypothesis can only provide a *trigger,* encouraging an incipient earthquake to burst into activity. This relatively small effect will not, on its own, cause an earthquake anywhere; it merely encourages earthquakes that would happen in any case to concentrate in a span of a few years around the time of the alignment.

The lack of any positive evidence of activity along the San Andreas at the beginning of the nineteenth century does not mean that our theory is necessarily wrong, although it would certainly give our ideas at least a small boost if any such evidence did turn up. So you can imagine our reaction when one of us came across just such evidences on a visit to California in October, 1974.

This visit (by JG) naturally involved a tour along part of the San Andreas fault, visiting sites of historic damage and regions of continual creep, including the small township of San Juan Bautista, which is just on the boundary of the active and quiescent parts of the fault near San Francisco. The area to the northwest of San Juan Bautista is both the southernmost locality where the ground was torn apart by the earthquake of 1906, and the northernmost region of continual creep. Quite apart from this interest, however, the mission at San Juan Bautista (which was severely damaged in 1906) is the oldest Californian mission to have been in continual use since it was founded; and the foundation took place in 1797.

After visiting the clearly apparent line of the fault itself, a visit to the mission was definitely in order— and proved doubly rewarding. The leaflet describing points of interest from the mission's history naturally includes mention of the 1906 earthquake, which caused the collapse of the outer walls of the church. But it also mentions an earlier period of earthquake activity: "In 1800, between October 11th and October 31st there were as many as 6 shocks per day." This earthquake is listed on p. 155 of the official "Earthquake History of the United States," U.S. Department of Commerce Publication 41-1, National Oceanic and Atmospheric Administration Environmental Data Service (1973). In addition to the earthquake at San Juan Bautista, the NOAA publication notes another major shock on November 22, 1800 in the San Diego Area which damaged the walls of adobe buildings at barracks in San Diego and cracked walls of a new church under construction at San Juan Capistrano. At

Santa Barbara in 1800 a violent quake was felt. Thus we have a record of at least three intermediate size earthquakes near the grand alignment of 1803. This is the only earthquake activity, apart from that of 1906, great enough to merit inclusion in the list of points of interest.

Our interest in this activity of the year 1800 can be imagined. The date does not quite fit with the exact date of the last planetary alignment (1803), but, as we have already mentioned, it is not clear whether it is the exact alignment or some equally rare configuration of the planets in the years building up to the alignment that provides the trigger; and if a fault is ready to go, the steadily increasing level of activity caused by the alignment effect could set it off even before the maximum trigger effect was produced. Arguments about earthquakes in the nineteenth century do not have much weight if we wish to compare with sunspot activity in this century. The population sample is changing through the years as our gathering of earthquake records improves. An analogy would be drawing 10 red and black beads from a jar every year, while all the time adding more red beads to the jar. You cannot compare the first draw of red and black beads to draws made later.

Information about the activity of 1800 is very scarce, but it is clear from historical records that shocks occurred consistently for 20 days, often being sufficient to shake the mission and cause the church bells to ring. Cracks appeared in the ground close to the nearby Pajaro River (this helps to establish the intensity as reaching the range VII in the official NOAA compilation, see Table 2 page 137), but that is about all we know for sure.

This evidence, such as it is, does not, of course,

have any conclusive bearing on our idea of the planets as triggers of devastating earthquakes. It proves neither that the theory is right nor wrong. In this book, we have presented only the first outline of ideas, which need much more discussion and refinement; perhaps this evidence, such as it is, indicates that our planetary trigger operates best a few years before the grand alignment, in which case the expected major earthquake in southern California may occur even before the end of the present decade. Perhaps the occurrence of such noteworthy activity in 1800 was entirely coincidental. We shall never know for sure. But the events certainly provide food for thought and material for discussion; the next time anyone asks us that awkward question we shall be ready with the answer: "That's a good question. Have you heard what happened to the mission at San Juan Bautista in October of the year 1800?"

Index

Atlantic Ocean, 2, 3, 5, 8, 12
Aurorae, 66–69, 98

Baja California, 17, 27, 33, 72, 75–76

Calaveras Fault Zone, 36, 40
Camp Dix, 32–37
Cape Mendocino, 30, 40–43
Chandler Wobble, 53–57, 61, 71
Cholame, 33, 35–39
Continental Drift, 3–4, 15–16, 52
'Creep,' 40, 46, 47, 134

Earth core, 54, 96
  crust, 2, 10, 28, 48, 52, 54, 97
  magma, 17
  magnetic field, 11, 12, 68–69, 84, 96, 97
  mantle, 28, 96
Earth's spin and solar activity, 81–95
Earth's spin and weather, 52–69
Earthquakes, damage, 133–48
  historic, 133, 134
  Los Angeles, 1857, 34, 39, 42, 132, 146–47
  San Fernando 1971, 38, 42, 139
  San Francisco 1906, 1, 36, 38, 41, 57, 132, 136, 143

Faults, strike-slip, 16, 32, 35, 37–38
  stick-slip, 47–48, 49–50, 134, 139
Flow, 46
Forbush Decreases, 87
Fracturing, 44–51

Gabbro, 49
Galapagos Volcanoes, 78–80
Garlock Fault, 18
Gondwanaland, 5, 7
Granite, 49

Hollister, 34, 35, 40
Hooke's Law, 44
Hornblende & Biotite, 49

Jerk, 2, 19, 32, 45

Laurasia, 3, 7, 8
Los Angeles, 17, 42, 132, 140, 146–48, 151
Lubrication (of faults), 50, 52, 78

Magnetism, 10–11
  Earth's, 11–13
  fossil, 11
  as recorder, 8–14, 28, 66
  reversals, 11, 66
Mercalli scale, 137–39
Monterey Bay, 34
Moonquakes, 76–77

Nutation, 54

Ocean ridge, 15–17, 22, 27, 75
Ocean trench, 9, 15, 16, 27

Package disaster hospitals, 141
Parkfield, 32–37
Planetary alignments and sun-
    spots, 108–32
Plates, 2, 15–16, 18–20, 30,
    45–48, 52, 75–76, 100,
    148
Polar movement, 53–57
Pole Star, 53–54, 66

Reid's elastic rebound theory,
    22
Richter's scale, 138

San Bernardino Mountains,
    18, 27, 39
San Francisco, 39, 40, 41, 42,
    133–48
San Gabriel Mountains, 17, 38

Seafloor spreading, 8–9, 12,
    20, 30
Seismology, 15
Sierra Nevada, 17
Solar flares, 81–95
Solar System, 52, 85, 89, 92–
    93, 98–107
Solar wind, 65–67, 85, 96
Stream channels, 32–37
Sunspots and Earth spin, 65,
    81–95
    and seismic activity, 78–79,
    99, 147
    and weather, 64–65, 66–70,
    148, 153–63
    and planetary alignments,
    108–32, 148, 152

Tectonics, see plates
Tides, 58, 71–80
    and the weather, 104–7
    on the Sun, 108–32

Viscoelasticity, 44–51

About the authors

JOHN R. GRIBBIN is an editor of *Nature,* the international journal of science published in London. He received his doctorate in astrophysics at Cambridge University in England. Dr. Gribbin lives with his wife and young son in Brighton, England.

STEPHEN PLAGEMANN, a physics major at the University of California at Berkeley, went on to receive his doctorate in 1971 at Cambridge University, where he worked at the Institute of Theoretical Astronomy under the eminent astronomer Sir Fred Hoyle. Dr. Plagemann has worked on special projects for the U.S. Geological Survey and for NASA. He now lives in England.

VINTAGE WOMEN'S STUDIES

V-72   BERNIKOW, LOUISE (ed.) / The World Split Open: Four Centuries of Women Poets in England and America, 1552-1950

V-227   DE BEAUVOIR, SIMONE / The Second Sex

V-359   DeCROW, KAREN / Sexist Justice

V-642   GLUCK, SHERNA (ed.) / From Parlor to Prison: Five American Suffragists Talk About Their Lives

V-407   HARDWICK, ELIZABETH / Seduction and Betrayal: Women and Literature

V-896   HATCH, JAMES AND VICTORIA SULLIVAN (eds.) / Plays By and About Women

V-880   LERNER, GERDA / Black Women in White America: A Documentary History

V-685   LESSING, DORIS / A Small Personal Voice: Essays, Reviews, Interviews

V-422   MITCHELL, JULIET / Psychoanalysis and Feminism

V-905   MITCHELL, JULIET / Woman's Estate

V-851   MORGAN, ROBIN / Monster

V-539   MORGAN, ROBIN (ed.) / Sisterhood Is Powerful: An Anthology of Writings from the Women's Liberation Movement

V-151   MOFFAT, MARY JANE AND CHARLOTTE PAINTER (eds.) / Revelations: Diaries of Women

V-960   OAKLEY, ANN / Woman's Work: The Housewife, Past and Present

V-151   PAINTER, CHARLOTTE AND MARY JANE MOFFAT (eds.) / Revelations: Diaries of Women

V-621   ROWBOTHAM, SHEILA / Hidden From History: Rediscovering Women in History from the 17th Century to the Present

V-954   ROWBOTHAM, SHEILA / Women, Resistance and Revolution: A History of Women and Revolution in the Modern World

V-41   SARGENT, PAMELA (ed.) / Women of Wonder: Science Fiction Stories by Women about Women

V-738   SCHNEIR, MIRIAM (ed.) / Feminism

V-806   SHERFEY, MARY JANE / The Nature and Evolution of Female Sexuality

V-896   SULLIVAN, VICTORIA AND JAMES HATCH (eds.) / Plays By and About Women

VINTAGE HISTORY—WORLD

V-286	**ARIES, PHILIPPE /** Centuries of Childhood
V-563	**BEER, SAMUEL H. /** British Politics in the Collectivist Age
V-620	**BILLINGTON, JAMES H. /** Icon and Axe: An Interpretive History of Russian Culture
V-44	**BRINTON, CRANE /** The Anatomy of Revolution
V-391	**CARR, E. H. /** What Is History?
V-628	**CARTEY, WILFRED AND MARTIN KILSON (eds.) /** Africa Reader: Colonial Africa, Vol. I
V-629	**CARTEY, WILFRED AND MARTIN KILSON (eds.) /** Africa Reader: Independent Africa, Vol. I
V-522	**CHINWEIZU /** The West and the Rest of Us: White Predators, Black Slavers and the African Elite
V-888	**CLARK, JOHN HENRIK (ed.) /** Marcus Garvey and the Vision of Africa
V-507	**CLIVE, JOHN /** Macauley
V-261	**COHEN, STEPHEN F. /** Bukharin and the Bolshevik Revolution: A Political Biography
V-843	**DAUBIER, JEAN /** A History of the Chinese Cultural Revolution
V-227	**DE BEAUVOIR, SIMONE /** The Second Sex
V-726	**DEBRAY, REGIS AND SALVADOR ALLENDE /** The Chilean Revolution
V-746	**DEUTSCHER, ISAAC /** The Prophet Armed
V-747	**DEUTSCHER, ISAAC /** The Prophet Outcast
V-748	**DEUTSCHER, ISAAC /** The Prophet Outcast
V-617	**DEVLIN, BERNADETTE /** The Price of My Soul
V-471	**DUVEAU, GEORGES /** 1848: The Making of A Revolution
V-702	**EMBREE, AINSLIE (ed.) /** The Hindu Tradition
V-2023	**FEST, JOACHIM C.** Hitler
V-225	**FISCHER, LOUIS /** The Essential Gandhi
V-927	**FITZGERALD, FRANCES /** Fire in the Lake: The Vietnamese & The Americans in Vietnam
V-914	**FOUCAULT, MICHEL /** Madness & Civilization: A History of Insanity in the Age of Reason
V-935	**FOUCAULT, MICHEL /** The Order of Things: An Archaeology of the Human Sciences
V-97	**FOUCAULT, MICHEL /** The Birth of the Clinic: An Archaeology of Medical Perception
V-152	**GRAHAM, LOREN R. /** Science & Philosophy in the Soviet Union
V-529	**HALLIDAY, FRED /** Arabia Without Sultans
V-114	**HAUSER, ARNOLD /** The Social History of Art (four volumes—through 117)
V-979	**HERZEN, ALEXANDER /** My Past and Thoughts (Abridged by Dwight Macdonald)
V-465	**HINTON, WILLIAM /** Fanshen
V-328	**HINTON, WILLIAM /** Iron Oxen
V-2005	**HOARE, QUINTIN (ed.) AND KARL MARX /** Early Writings
V-878	**HOLBORN, HAJO (ed.) /** Republic to Reich: The Making of the Nazi Revolution

V-201   HUGHES, H. STUART / Consciousness and Society
V-514   HUNTINGTON, SAMUEL P. / The Soldier and the State
V-790   KAPLAN, CAROL AND LAWRENCE / Revolutions: A Comparative Study
V-708   KESSLE, GUN AND JAN MYRDAL / China: The Revolution Continued
V-628   KILSON, MARTIN AND WILFRED CARTEY (eds.) / Africa Reader: Colonial Africa, Vol. I
V-629   KILSON, MARTIN AND WILFRED CARTEY (eds.) / Africa Reader: Independent Africa, Vol. II
V-728   KLYUCHEVSKY, V. / Peter the Great
V-246   KNOWLES, DAVID / Evolution of Medieval Thought
V-939   LEFEBVRE, GEORGES AND JOAN WHITE (trans.) / The Great Fear of 1789: Rural Panic in Revolutionary France
V-754   LIEBMAN, MARCEL / The Russian Revolution
V-533   LOCKWOOD, LEE / Castro's Cuba, Cuba's Fidel
V-787   MALDONADO-DENIS, MANUEL / Puerto Rico: A Socio-Historic Interpretation
V-406   MARCUS, STEVEN / Engels, Manchester & The Working Class
V-480   MARCUSE, HERBERT / Soviet Marxism
V-2002 MARX, KARL AND DAVID FERNBACH (ed.) / Political Writings, Vol. I: The Revolutions of 1848
V-2003 MARX, KARL AND DAVID FERNBACH (ed.) / Political Writings, Vol. II: Surveys from Exile
V-2004 MARX, KARL AND DAVID FERNBACH (ed.) / Political Writings, Vol. III: The First International and After
V-2005 MARX, KARL AND QUINTIN HOARE (ed.) / Early Writings
V-2001 MARX, KARL AND MARTIN NICOLOUS (trans.) / Grundrisse: Foundations of the Critique of Political Economy
V-92   MATTINGLY, GARRETT / Catherine of Aragon
V-928   MEDVEDEV, ROY A. / Let History Judge: The Origins & Consequences of Stalinism
V-816   MEDVEDEV, ROY & ZHORES / A Question of Madness
V-112   MEDVEDEV, ZHORES / Ten Years After Ivan Denisovich
V-971   MILTON, DAVID & NANCY AND FRANZ SCHURMANN / The China Reader IV: People's China:
V-905   MITCHELL, JULIET / Woman's Estate
V-730   MYRDAL, GUNNAR / Asian Drama: An Inquiry into the Poverty of Nations
V-793   MYRDAL, JAN / Report from a Chinese Village
V-708   MYRDAL, JAN AND GUN KESSLE / China: The Revolution Continued
V-2001 NICOLOUS, MARTIN (trans.) AND KARL MARX / The Grundrisse: Foundations of the Critique of Political Economy
V-955   O'BRIEN, CONOR CRUISE / States of Ireland
V-689   OBSERVER, AN / Message From Moscow
V-525   PARES, SIR BERNARD / A History of Russia
V-719   REED, JOHN / Ten Days That Shook the World
V-677   RODINSON, MAXIME / Mohammed
V-954   ROWBOTHAM, SHEILA / Women, Resistance & Revolution: A History of Women & Revolution in the Modern World
V-2067 SAKHAROV, ANDREI / My Country and The World

V-303   SANSOM, GEORGE B. / The Western World & Japan
V-745   SCHAPIRO, LEONARD / The Communist Party of the Soviet Union
V-738   SCHNEIR, MIRIAM (ed.) / Feminism
V-375   SCHURMANN, F. AND O. SCHELL (eds.) / The China Reader, Vol. I: Imperial China
V-376   SCHURMANN, F. AND O. SCHELL (eds.) / The China Reader, Vol. II: Republican China
V-377   SCHURMANN, F. AND O. SCHELL (eds.) / The China Reader, Vol. III: Communist China
V-971   SCHURMANN, F. AND DAVID & NANCY MILTON / The China Reader, Vol. IV: People's China
V-405   SERVICE, JOHN S. AND JOSEPH H. ESHERICK (ed.) / Lost Chance in China: The World War II Despatches of John S. Service
V-847   SNOW, EDGAR / Journey to the Beginning
V-930   SNOW, EDGAR / The Long Revolution
V-681   SNOW, EDGAR / Red China Today: The Other Side of the River
V-220   SOBOUL, ALBERT / The French Revolution, 1787-1799: From the Storming of the Bastille to Napoleon
V-411   SPENCE, JONATHAN / Emperor of China: Self-Portait of K'ang-hsi
V-962   STERN, FRITZ / The Varieties of History: From Voltaire to the Present
V-312   TANNENBAUM, FRANK / Ten Keys to Latin America
V-387   TAYLOR, A. J. P. / Bismark: The Man and the Statesman
V-322   THOMPSON, E. P. / The Making of the English Working Class
V-298   WATTS, ALAN / The Way of Zen
V-939   WHITE, JOAN (trans.) AND GEORGES LEFEBVRE / The Great Fear of 1789: Rural Panic in Revolutionary France
V-627   WOMACK, John Jr. / Zapata and the Mexican Revolution

VINTAGE BELLES—LETTRES

V-418   AUDEN, W. H. / The Dyer's Hand
V-887   AUDEN, W. H. / Forewords and Afterwords
V-271   BEDIER, JOSEPH / Tristan and Iseult
V-512   BLOCH, MARC / The Historian's Craft
V-572   BRIDGEHAMPTON / Bridgehampton Works & Days
V-161   BROWN, NORMAN O. / Closing Time
V-544   BROWN, NORMAN O. / Hermes the Thief
V-419   BROWN, NORMAN O. / Love's Body
V-75   CAMUS, ALBERT / The Myth of Sisyphus and Other Essays
V-30   CAMUS, ALBERT / The Rebel
V-608   CARR, JOHN DICKSON / The Life of Sir Arthur Conan Doyle: The Man Who Was Sherlock Holmes
V-407   HARDWICK, ELIZABETH / Seduction and Betrayal: Women and Literature
V-244   HERRIGEL, EUGEN / The Method of Zen
V-663   HERRIGEL, EUGEN / Zen in the Art of Archery
V-201   HUGHES, H. STUART / Consciousness & Society
V-235   KAPLAN, ABRAHAM / New World of Philosophy
V-337   KAUFMANN, WALTER (trans.) AND FRIEDRICH NIETZSCHE / Beyond Good and Evil
V-369   KAUFMANN, WALTER (trans.) AND FRIEDRICH NIETZSCHE / The Birth of Tragedy and the Case of Wagner
V-985   KAUFMANN, WALTER (trans.) AND FRIEDRICH NIETZSCHE / The Gay Science
V-401   KAUFMANN, WALTER (trans.) AND FRIEDRICH NIETZSCHE / On the Genealogy of Morals and Ecce Homo
V-437   KAUFMANN, WALTER (trans.) AND FRIEDRICH NIETZSCHE / The Will to Power
V-995   KOTT, JAN / The Eating of the Gods: An Interpretation of Greek Tragedy
V-685   LESSING, DORIS / A Small Personal Voice: Essays, Reviews, Interviews
V-329   LINDBERGH, ANNE MORROW / Gift from the Sea
V-479   MALRAUX, ANDRE / Man's Fate
V-406   MARCUS, STEVEN / Engels, Manchester and the Working Class
V-58   MENCKEN, H. L. / Prejudices (Selected by James T. Farrell)
V-25   MENCKEN, H. L. / The Vintage Mencken (Gathered by Alistair Cooke)
V-151   MOFFAT, MARY JANE AND CHARLOTTE PAINTER (eds.) / Revelations: Diaries of Women
V-926   MUSTARD, HELEN (trans.) / Heinrich Heine: Selected Works
V-337   NIETZSCHE, FRIEDRICH AND WALTER KAUFMANN (trans.) / Beyond Good and Evil
V-369   NIETZSCHE, FRIEDRICH AND WALTER KAUFMANN (trans.) / The Birth of Tragedy and the Case of Wagner
V-985   NIETZSCHE, FRIEDRICH AND WALTER KAUFMANN (trans.) / The Gay Science
V-401   NIETZSCHE, FRIEDRICH AND WALTER KAUFMANN (trans.) / On the Genealogy of Morals and Ecce Homo

V-437 NIETZSCHE, FRIEDRICH AND WALTER KAUFMANN (trans.) / The Will to Power
V-672 OUSPENSKY, P. D. / The Fourth Way
V-524 OUSPENSKY, P. D. / A New Model of the Universe
V-943 OUSPENSKY, P. D. / The Psychology of Man's Possible Evolution
V-639 OUSPENSKY, P. D. / Tertium Organum
V-151 PAINTER, CHARLOTTE AND MARY JANE MOFFAT (eds.) / Revelations: Diaries of Women
V-986 PAUL, DAVID (trans.) / Poison & Vision: Poems & Prose of Baudelaire, Mallarme and Rimbaud
V-598 PROUST, MARCEL / The Captive
V-597 PROUST, MARCEL / Cities of the Plain
V-596 PROUST, MARCEL / The Guermantes Way
V-594 PROUST, MARCEL / Swann's Way
V-599 PROUST, MARCEL / The Sweet Cheat Gone
V-595 PROUST, MARCEL / Within a Budding Grove
V-899 SAMUEL, MAURICE / The World of Sholom Aleichem
V-415 SHATTUCK, ROGER / The Banquet Years (revised)
V-278 STEVENS, WALLACE / The Necessary Angel
V-761 WATTS, ALAN / Behold the Spirit
V-923 WATTS, ALAN / Beyond Theology: The Art of Godmanship
V-853 WATTS, ALAN / The Book: the Taboo Against Knowing Who You Are
V-999 WATTS, ALAN / Cloud-Hidden, Whereabouts Unknown: A Mountain Journal
V-665 WATTS, ALAN / Does It Matter?
V-951 WATTS, ALAN / In My Own Way
V-299 WATTS, ALAN / The Joyous Cosmology
V-592 WATTS, ALAN / Nature, Man and Woman
V-609 WATTS, ALAN / Psychotherapy East & West
V-835 WATTS, ALAN / The Supreme Identity
V-298 WATTS, ALAN / The Way of Zen
V-870 WIESEL, ELIE / Souls on Fire